# SACRED GROUND

# SACRED GROUND

## PLURALISM, PREJUDICE, AND
## THE PROMISE OF AMERICA

Eboo Patel

BEACON PRESS
BOSTON

Beacon Press
25 Beacon Street
Boston, Massachusetts 02108-2892
www.beacon.org

Beacon Press books
are published under the auspices of
the Unitarian Universalist Association of Congregations.

15   14   13   12      8   7   6   5   4   3   2   1

This book is printed on acid-free paper that meets the uncoated paper
ANSI/NISO specifications for permanence as revised in 1992.

Text design and composition by Wilsted & Taylor Publishing Services

Library of Congress Cataloging-in-Publication Data
Patel, Eboo.
Sacred ground : pluralism, prejudice, and the promise
of America / Eboo Patel.
p. cm.
Includes bibliographical references and index.
ISBN 978-0-8070-7748-1 (hardcover: alk. paper)
1. Religious pluralism—United States.  2. Religions—Relations.
3. Islam—Relations.  4. United States—Religions.  I. Title.
BL2525.P36 2012
204'.50973—dc23                              2012013687

*To the leaders,*
*to the bridge builders*

*May the Father of all mercies scatter light and not darkness in our paths, and make us all in our several vocations useful here, and in His own due time and way everlastingly happy.*

—George Washington

*The good we secure for ourselves is precarious and uncertain until it is secured for all of us and incorporated into our common life.*

—Jane Addams

# CONTENTS

# INTRODUCTION

If only they knew about Cordoba.

It was 2009. I was in my office at Interfaith Youth Core, clicking through a recently released Pew Research Center study on religion, racking my brain for new strategies. Eight years after 9/11, the survey said, a majority of Americans—65 percent—viewed Islam as very or somewhat different from their own religion.[1] Fewer than one in five of my fellow citizens thought that my faith had anything in common with theirs. It raised a question that had been nagging me deep down for some time: For all the growth in the numbers of people committed to making faith a bridge of cooperation, was our movement any match for those who saw faith as a barrier of division or a bomb of destruction? The evening news was still full of stories of suicide bombings in Iraq and Afghanistan, books like Christopher Hitchens's *God Is Not Great: How Religion Poisons Everything* were runaway best sellers, and chain e-mails with headings like "Why Muslims Can't Be Good Americans" were landing in my in-box on a regular basis. All of this was proof that interfaith work was not taking place on neutral territory. There were plenty of people out there with a very different idea about religious diversity, and they were not shy.

The work of Interfaith Youth Core (IFYC), the nonprofit organization I founded and have led for the last ten years, focuses on training young people from different faiths to organize interfaith service projects. The idea is that serving others is a common value to all traditions—including secular ones—and when religiously diverse young people engage in volunteer projects together, they become both committed to the cause of interfaith cooperation and ambassadors for its importance. I was coming to the realization that these activities were necessary but not sufficient. We needed new strategies, new approaches that could give rise to a new narrative, a tale that spanned the ages and included people of all religions and cultures, a story about the magnificence of putting the high ideals of pluralism into concrete practice.

That's where Cordoba came in. It was the capital city of Al-Andalus, an Islamic civilization in southern Spain in the medieval era, a time of Muslim rule characterized by cooperation with Jews and Christians often referred to as La Convivencia. "The brilliant ornament of the world [that] shone in the west," the cultivated Catholic nun Hroswitha called it, "a noble city . . . wealthy and famous . . . and resplendent in all things, and especially for its seven streams of wisdom and as much for its constant victories."[2] The library of the caliph had four hundred thousand volumes, a thousand times more than the largest library in the Christian-dominated parts of Europe. The catalogue of the library alone ran to forty-four volumes. Jews, hounded and hated elsewhere in Europe, thrived here. This was the milieu that gave rise to the great Jewish philosopher Maimonides, where Hebrew poetry was rediscovered and reinvented, where a Jew rose to be the Caliph's foreign minister. While much of Europe was experiencing the Dark Ages, Muslim scholars were producing commentaries on Aristotle, texts that played a key role in sparking the Renaissance in Europe. The influence of Al-Andalus is with us still: there are synagogues on New York City's Upper West Side with architectural allusions to the mosques built in that time and place.[3]

Here was a Muslim society that promoted art and science, medicine and mathematics, literature and philosophy, values and disciplines admired across nations and religions. If more of my fellow citizens knew about Cordoba, certainly they would see similarities between Islam and America. Moreover, they might start to glimpse the arc of that narrative of pluralism, and see themselves as authors of future chapters.

The Cordoba story has been frequently mentioned in academic circles. Yale professor Maria Rosa Menocal wrote *The Ornament of the World: How Muslims, Jews, and Christians Created a Culture of Tolerance in Medieval Spain*, and Harvard professor Diana Eck had referenced La Convivencia in her presidential address to the American Academy of Religion, the largest association of religion scholars in North America. My own introduction to Cordoba was in my graduate studies in the sociology of religion. It was my inspiration for starting an interfaith organization. I wanted to be deep in the mix when it came to cultivating pluralism. My wife and I took a trip to southern Spain to see the mosques and monuments for ourselves, to follow in the footsteps of our ancestors who had built a civilization we took pride in. And while I was there, it occurred to me that the most powerful similarity between medieval Andalusia and contemporary America wasn't in the architecture of the buildings; it was in the shape of the society—namely, the idea that different religious communities can live in the same place and not simply coexist in a lukewarm tolerance, but rather actively cooperate and mutually thrive.

In *What It Means to Be an American,* Michael Walzer observes that political theorists since the Greeks believed that participatory politics could exist only in ethnically or religiously homogenous nations: "One religious communion, it was argued, made one political community . . . One people made one state." Pluralism—one state with many peoples—existed only under empires. The next section begins with this line: "Except in the United States."[4]

Cordoba predicted America. It was a civilization that experimented with a partial pluralism, extended limited rights to diverse communities, and allowed some degree of civic and political participation. The American story is about the adoption and advancement of all three principles.

Human history is littered with examples of different identity groups at war with each other. More frequently than the faithful would like to admit, religious belief has fueled the fighting. Against this backdrop, the American achievement, while far from perfect, is still remarkable. As Barack Obama said in his inaugural address, "Our patchwork heritage is a strength, not a weakness. We are a nation of Christians and Muslims, Jews and Hindus, and nonbelievers. We are shaped by every language and culture, drawn from every end of this Earth."[5] What is even more astonishing is our refusal to stand still, to be content with past progress or favorable comparisons to other nations. We constantly seek to improve this pluralist, participatory, patchwork democracy.

America's promise is to guarantee equal rights for all identities. This framework of rights facilitates the contributions of these many communities to this single country. That is America's genius. The idea is simple: people whose nation gives them dignity will build up that society. When we say we are an immigrant nation, we mean more than just that various religious and ethnic groups settled here in America, bringing with them their Hebrew prayers and Hindu chants. We are recognizing the fact that the institutions they built benefited not just their own communities but also the common good of this country. The hyphen between Jewish, Christian, and American is not a barrier; it's a bridge. Those things that make you a better Catholic or Buddhist or Sikh—generosity, compassion, service—also make you a better American. America gains when its immigrants bring the inspiration of their particular heritage across the ocean to these shores and plant it in this soil. Those seeds have grown into Catholic hospitals, Lutheran colleges, Quaker high schools, Southern Baptist disaster-relief organizations, Jewish philanthropy, and much more. The institutional expressions of religious identity are the engines of American civil society. These were lessons I learned not from a political science seminar in college but from a Muslim imam from Egypt.

Perhaps it is fitting that I first saw Imam Feisal Abdul Rauf speak at New York City's Riverside Church, where forty years earlier Martin Luther King Jr. had preached about how his Christian faith called him to be an interfaith peace builder.[6] Dressed in a dignified silver Arab robe, looking perfectly comfortable in front of a multicultural Christian congregation, Imam Feisal opened with the line, "My dear brothers and sisters, I bring you greetings of peace from the tradition of Islam." In a calm, gentle voice—a voice that my IFYC colleague Claire said made her want to do yoga—he spoke of his devotion to both Islam and America. He had lived in the Middle East, in Europe, in Malaysia, and had never felt so free and welcome as he did here, in a nation whose principles are totally congruous with the values of his faith, a country that inspired him to do his best work.

For Imam Feisal, the great fault line in the world is not between Americans and Arabs or Muslims and Christians. It is between the moderates of all traditions and the extremists who belong only to one—the tradition of extremism. It was a fault line Imam Feisal knew well. His father had once been kidnapped by Muslim extremists, and his own mosque was in Lower Manhattan, only a few blocks from where fanatics from his faith rammed planes into the World Trade Center. The gun of religious violence had been pointed at his chest many times, more often than not by people who prayed in Arabic.

Imam Feisal loved to highlight the dimensions of pluralism in every tradition. In Islam, he cited the verses of the Qur'an and the sayings of the Prophet Muhammad. He spoke of those seeds flowering into the glorious civilization of Al-Andalus. He called New York City a contemporary Cordoba, sacred ground where God's multitudes mingled and mixed, a city to be cherished and protected. I remember feeling a flush of pride when Imam Feisal spoke those words. As an American Muslim, I was part of both stories.

Many Muslim leaders of the immigrant generation, while grateful for America's freedoms and opportunities, openly registered their disapproval of American popular culture and foreign policy. They spoke often of life back home, offering heavily mythologized versions of mid-twentieth century

Karachi or Cairo, and set out to repeat those patterns here. They built a set of institutions—mosques, schools, advocacy organizations—whose purpose was to seal Muslims off from much of American cultural life, institutions that served as bubbles rather than bridges. Imam Feisal was saying something different. He spoke of how Catholicism and Judaism had become American religions by bursting out of their bubbles, learning from and working with others, and building institutions that served the common good of their new country instead of just the concerns of their own parochial communities. Muslims ought to do the same, he insisted. We could maintain our distinctive identities while contributing to the civic life of our nation. America welcomed that. Look at the popularity of Rumi's poetry and the iconic status of Muhammad Ali. Gaze up at the heights of the Sears Tower, a building designed by an American Muslim. Integrating the distinct contributions of its diverse religious communities is the American way. This is the true meaning of *E pluribus unum*. This is how this nation was built.

Imam Feisal's great dream was to create an institution that embodied this ideal. It would be something analogous to a YMCA (the initials of which stand for "Young Men's *Christian* Association") or a Jewish Community Center, a project that made reference to the Islamic tradition and harnessed the resources of the Muslim community with the purpose of serving the common good of this country. It would be the institutional expression of Muslim pluralism and service in America. He planned to name it after the city that had embodied this ethos in a Muslim civilization many centuries before: Cordoba House.

It was a vision that inspired me to go see Imam Feisal speak a dozen times, at events in cities ranging from DC to London. And I wasn't the only one. Imam Feisal was among the most sought-after figures at interfaith conferences across the world in the years after 9/11. He was everywhere—at churches and synagogues, at Aspen Institute events and State Department conferences, at Muslim youth gatherings and at the World Economic Forum, in Davos. I remember receiving a call from a man who was planning a major interfaith conference in Washington, DC, a man who had served as a senior official in the Bush administration. The man simply said, "You've got to help us get Imam Feisal for this conference. People are saying they won't come unless he speaks."

When I saw the article in the *New York Times* in early December 2009, I smiled widely and thought to myself, "He's making it happen." Imam Feisal had found a building for Cordoba House, and it was only a few blocks from the mosque where he had led prayers and given sermons for twenty-five years. The finished project would include a 500-seat performing arts center, a gym, a restaurant, a library, a culinary school, a swimming pool, and a prayer space. Muslims would take their place alongside other American communities as a group that built an institution out of the inspiration of their particular heritage in a manner that served their nation.

The project's real estate developer, a Muslim who prayed at Imam Feisal's mosque, stated the intention of the project: "It's really to provide a place of peace, a place of services and solutions for the community."[1] The *Times* quoted a half-dozen people who supported the effort, from government officials to religious leaders to people who had lost loved ones in the 9/11 attacks. A spokeswoman for the National September 11 Memorial and Museum said, "The idea of a cultural center that strengthens ties between Muslims and people of all faiths and backgrounds is positive." An FBI staffer told the *Times*, "We've had positive interactions with him in the past." A woman whose son was killed on 9/11 called it "a noble effort."

The closest parallel to Cordoba House was Manhattan's Jewish Community Center, and Imam Feisal and his wife, Daisy Khan, reached out to them for advice. Joy Levitt, the center's executive director, was quoted in the *Times* article as saying, "For the J.C.C. to have partners in the Muslim community who share our vision of pluralism and tolerance would be great." She did give Imam Feisal and Daisy some stern advice: Leave enough space for baby strollers.[8]

There were some brief references to the "delicate nature" of the project in the *Times* piece, given that it was going to be near Ground Zero, where a group of extremist Muslims had murdered nearly three thousand Americans. If anybody could pull this off, the article suggested, it would be Imam Feisal. Not only was he a figure with significant national clout, he led a mosque right in the neighborhood. His own Muslim community had been deeply impacted by the tragedy. The *Times* wasn't the only media that leaned positive on the project. In late 2009, the conservative commentator Laura Ingraham, hosted Daisy on Fox News and declared her support. It looked like clear sailing.[9]

There was one thing that made me nervous—the swimming pool. "That's going to be trouble," I thought to myself. Imam Feisal had always been viewed as a little too liberal by certain contingents within American Islam. Even the *Times* story mentioned that Imam Feisal had a tendency to be "focused more on cultivating relations with those outside the faith than within it." Imam Feisal's unabashed affection for America, his work with the US government on the issue of domestic Muslim extremism, his willingness to be identified as a moderate Muslim, all these things had caused grumbling within some segments of his own community. Many wanted more criticism of US foreign policy and popular culture, and just about everyone wanted Imam Feisal to tell all his powerful friends to stop using the term "moderate Muslim." They thought it signified that the US government could tell Muslims how to practice their religion.

Personally, I could live with the term. The Qur'an says that Muslims were meant to be a community in the middle, and if that translated into American English as "moderate Muslim"—fine.[10] Plus, given the high-profile nature of Muslim terrorists, I thought the biggest challenge for American Muslims was to redirect the spotlight toward people like

Imam Feisal and historical moments like Cordoba and away from the suicide bombers of al-Qaeda.

Oh, for the days when we argued about the term "moderate Muslim." By the end of that summer, it had effectively ceased to exist.

The first punch to land was from Pamela Geller, a right-wing blogger and well-known flamethrower. In May 2010, she posted a piece referring to Cordoba House as a "Victory Mosque at Ground Zero." The language was picked up by the *New York Post* and started getting traction on Fox News and other conservative outlets. Sarah Palin tweeted that Muslims should "refudiate" Cordoba House. The lieutenant governor of Tennessee said that Muslims could well be part of a cult and therefore undeserving of First Amendment rights. Political candidates from Nevada to North Carolina started making their opposition to "the Ground Zero mosque" a core part of their campaign strategy. Mosque projects from the suburbs of San Diego to Staten Island—literally, from sea to shining sea—faced vociferous opposition. A group of young men in a car fired several shots at Muslim worshippers leaving a mosque in upstate New York. A mosque construction site in Murfreesboro, Tennessee, was hit by an arson attack. A cab driver in Manhattan was asked if he was Muslim, said yes, and got stabbed four times. An obscure pastor in Florida with a Hollywood mustache started making news with his announcement that on September 11 he was going to burn Qur'ans. On Fox News, Imam Feisal was known simply as the radical Imam building a victory mosque on the site where his terrorist brethren had committed the worst attack in American history.

Much of this occurred during Ramadan, which ran from mid-August to mid-September that year. I would read the stories in early morning, around five a.m., right after I ate a small meal, drank a glass of water, and said the prayers that began my day of fasting. Under normal circumstances, I would have spent the time between opening my fast and going to work reading Rumi poems and verses of the Qur'an. God listens closely during the dawn hours, we Muslims believe. But not this Ramadan. Instead of centering myself spiritually, I was on one anti-Muslim blog after another, trying to anticipate the media story line of the day. Any new attacks on Imam Feisal? Any more Muslims getting shot at?

That's when I saw my name: "Eboo Patel, radical Muslim." I scrolled down. "Eboo Patel, Muslim extremist." I started clicking on other sites. "Eboo Patel, *Muslim terrorist.*" I was all over the anti-Muslim blogosphere. A few days earlier, I had talked with my friend Saleemah Abdul-Ghafur, and she had asked a question that I had no answer to: "There are Muslim imams out there who actually do hate America. Imam Feisal is not one of them. He *loves* America. So, why are these guys going after him?"

Looking at my name with the word *terrorist* next to it, I had a theory: My speeches and writings highlighted the shared values between Islam and America. My first book, *Acts of Faith*,[11] told the story of how I came to hold that view and how it was being put into practice in the work of Interfaith Youth Core. All of this had paved the path for President Obama to appoint me to his inaugural Faith Council. Having made an America-loving, well-spoken Muslim leader like Imam Feisal radioactive, the forces of intolerance were now seeking to set fire to anybody who could broadly be classified in the same category. These people were trying to send a very clear message: *We can take out even your most moderate, media-friendly, pro-American Muslim public figures. The rest of you better beware: We're coming for you next.* It was like a pitcher brushing back a batter. And if the ball happened to catch you in the knee? Oh, well, it's just part of the price you pay for being Muslim.

As irksome as the term "moderate Muslim" was, at least it recognized that there was a difference between the extremists and the rest of us. This discourse was different. It baldly claimed that Islam was inherently radical. The only moderate Muslims were the ones who repudiated their religion, and even then it took years for the poison to be fully purged from their systems. Voices pushing this view had existed on the fringe for some time. What made the summer of 2010 different is that these people broke through the fence and infected the mainstream, and they did it through an especially odious strategy. The old approach was to take marginal extremists and claim they represented the mainstream community—the Osama-bin-Laden-represents-all-Muslims' line. This time, they were doing something far more radical: They were taking a well-respected imam and painting him as a monster. They were taking the golden age of Islamic civilization and claiming it was an era of Islamist domination. They were talking about the Muslim equivalent of a YMCA as a terrorist command center. "Nothing that has ever been near Islam can be good" was their message. I had spent all this time organizing interfaith service projects. I thought it might have been working. I wish the worst of it was that I felt stupid. The truth is I felt like I'd been punched in the face.

My mother was nervous. In thirty-five years in America, she'd never been afraid of telling people she referred to God as Allah or fasted during Ramadan. But the summer of 2010 was too much for her. Some of her friends were acting a little strange. Previously, they had chattered happily about my media appearances on interfaith cooperation. But when I started speaking out against the prejudice directed at Muslims, I must have crossed a line, and some started giving my mom the cold shoulder. "But do you have to be so bold about it?" my mother asked when I told her that I wasn't going to shy away from calling out blatant bigotry. And then her voice changed.

"Eboo," she said, "I'm worried about your children."

"The kids are fine," I told her, "just high energy."

"I'm not worried about their energy," she said, "I'm worried about their names. They sound too Muslim. What will happen to them on the playground at school? Who will defend them from bullies? Even the teachers might treat them badly. They're young yet, Eboo—it's not too late to give them more American names. In a year, no one will remember their old names."

"Zayd and Khalil *are* American names," I told her. But I have to admit it made me wonder: How many of my fellow citizens viewed it the same way?

This was just election-year madness, my friends tried to assure me. After early November, Fox News would move on to other things. I just shook my head when I heard that. It's not like the 2010 election was the *last* one America was going to hold. If anti-Muslim messages worked for candidates this time around, what would stop them from using those messages next time? Plus, this was a midterm, a time when political parties test out messages in advance of the general election. My fear was that what we were witnessing was just a little prejudice rainstorm. The hurricane was still on the horizon. As the media conversation pivoted away from Cordoba House and became absorbed in the dangers that sharia law held for America well past the midterm, all I could say was, "I told you so." Another time, a different song, but the album was the same: "We Hate Muslims."

The irony of it all is that religious tolerance is viewed as part of American exceptionalism, even as an American export. The problems, we have long believed, lie *over there.* In the Middle East and South Asia, where religious groups continue to slaughter each other in the streets. In Europe, which simply can't get its head around how to integrate its growing Muslim population. I've been invited to all these places— glittering European capitals, Middle East palaces, universities in India. I've dispensed advice to royals and government officials, academic types and leaders of nongovernmental organizations, proudly sermonizing on the topic of "How We Americans Are Doing So Well at Managing Our Religious Diversity in This Era of Religious Conflict, and What We Can Teach the Rest of You."

But when push came to shove—when a small group of

hate-filled right wingers wanted to manufacture the Great Muslim Scare, to swift-boat a respected imam, to label a Muslim-inspired interfaith project in Lower Manhattan a terrorist command center, to encourage vociferous opposition to mosques around the country, to push anti-sharia referendums in two dozen states—they simply steamrolled us. They got themselves presented on respected television news shows as experts on Islam instead of as exemplars of bigotry. They were received by much of the public as American patriots rather than as ugly racists. If we were to score the summer of 2010, the forces of intolerance would have defeated the forces of inclusiveness in a blowout. Disgusted, I thought to myself: if I am invited back to those glittering European capitals or Middle East palaces anytime in the next few years, it will probably be to get laughed at. I was teetering between despair and rage.

And then I got a call from Shaykh Hamza Yusuf. Born Mark Hanson, he had changed his name when he converted to Islam as a young man. *Shaykh* is a title—not unlike *rabbi*—bestowed on an individual deeply learned in the tradition. Shaykh Hamza earned it during his many years of Islamic study in West Africa, and since returning to the United States, had become the Muslim community's most popular preacher and public intellectual. Tens of thousands of Muslims flock to attend his keynotes at conferences, eager to see a white man speaking perfect Arabic, eloquently holding forth on the harmonies between the glories of Islam and the promise of America, proving it by quoting the Qur'an and Bob Dylan with equal flow.

I was one of those admirers. I bought CDs of Shaykh Hamza's teachings and watched his sermons online. Like Imam Feisal, he was one of those intellectual and spiritual lights who viewed Islam and America as mutually enriching rather than mutually exclusive.

I met Shaykh Hamza at a program of American Muslim leaders focused on bridging the divide between Islam and the West a few years after 9/11. My assigned seat was next to his. He spent the entire day whispering somewhat irreverent commentary on the whole affair to me under his breath. After that, Shaykh Hamza took me under his wing, introducing me to other Muslim scholars and vouching for me in more traditionalist circles. Occasionally, I'd get a phone call from him. It was always out of the blue, and it was always short. He would tell me what he had to tell me, usually about a book he thought I needed to read or a conference I had to attend, and then he'd say, *"Salam alaykum"* and hang up. This time, he wanted to talk about the madness surrounding Muslims in the summer of 2010. I expected him to be despairing or angry, like me. But to my surprise, he had a very different view.

"Eeebooooo," he said in that unmistakable California drawl. *"Salam alaykum.* This is your brother Hamza. *Ramadan Kareem."*

*"Wa Alaykum As-Salam,* Shaykh Hamza. *Ramadan Kareem."*

"How are you doing?" he asked me.

Shaykh Hamza was never shy about offering his opinion if he thought something was going wrong, whether it was with his country or his religious community. I was happy to commiserate with him. "I'm angry, Shaykh Hamza," I told him. "I'm angry at what they're doing to Imam Feisal and Daisy. I don't know what's happening to my country. I feel like America *wants* to believe the worst things about Muslims, to fall for the ridiculous hatred of a handful of bigots."

Nothing could have surprised me more than what Shaykh Hamza said next: "That's the wrong response, Eboo. You're looking at this upside down. We Muslims have known these bigots have existed for a long time. Now the whole country knows. The traction they're getting is only temporary. God bless Daisy Khan and Imam Feisal, they have helped lift up a national discussion we've needed to have. These are the moments that change agents yearn for, Eboo. Our country is molten and can be shaped. Ask Allah to help you do your work well. This is Ramadan, and our nation needs it."

Shaykh Hamza was telling me to believe in America and do my best work? What was he talking about? *"Salam Alaykum,"* I heard him say. And then *click*, he was gone.

This book began in that moment—in the realization that there is no better time to stand up for your values than when they are under attack, that bigotry concealed doesn't go away, it only festers underground. It's only when the poison of prejudice emerges out in the open that it can be confronted directly.

This book is about the promise of American pluralism. In his essay "The Little Man at Chehaw Station," the great African American writer Ralph Ellison spoke on "the irrepressible movement of American culture towards integration of its most diverse elements continues, confounding the circumlocutions of its staunchest opponents." That statement is true only because people have made it true. There are many times in American history when the staunch opponents of American pluralism have won the battle. They didn't win the war because irrepressible people refused to forfeit their nation to these forces. Simply put, it is people who have protected the promise of pluralism from the poison of prejudice.

The first section of this book examines the battle over Cordoba House in the light of this history. Part of what gave Shaykh Hamza hope were the people who, at great risk to their own careers and reputations, came to the aid of Muslims in that dark hour. Yet part of what shocked me was the number of prominent figures only too happy to ride the wave of prejudice for personal gain. The first section profiles both types and traces a line from present times to past chapters in American history in which the forces of pluralism squared off against the forces of prejudice. Shaykh Hamza was right: Our nation was shaped by those battles.

Shaykh Hamza had told me to pray to God that I do my work well. His framing the challenge positively was a gesture of kindness. He could just as easily have pointed out that the Cordoba House episode showed that I had not done my work well enough. After all, the purpose of Interfaith Youth Core is to build understanding and cooperation between different faith communities. That went up in flames during the Cordoba House episode.

What does it mean to do interfaith work well? Frankly, that is a question I had rarely asked in the decade I'd been building Interfaith Youth Core. Moreover, it was a question I don't remember hearing very often in the fifteen years I'd been involved in the broader interfaith movement. We were constantly congratulating each other for simply doing the work, and we were positively vain about how fast the movement was growing. Conversations about effectiveness were commonplace in other fields: education, poverty alleviation, environmentalism. They were virtually nonexistent in interfaith work. Had we done our work better, could we have prevented the Cordoba House madness? If we improve our effectiveness, could we at least mitigate the next anti-whoever round of bigotry? I think we can, and the second part of this book shows how. I believe that there is a science of interfaith cooperation and an art to interfaith leadership and that if we apply these intelligently to key sectors of American life—I write specifically about colleges, seminaries, and parenting in the final section—the promise of pluralism will be much more secure.

Was everyone who opposed Cordoba House an outright bigot? Of course not. I can count several dozen people I consider friends and colleagues who had questions about the project. While I disagreed with them on this matter, their integrity is unimpeachable. They are most certainly the furthest thing from bigots. There is a huge difference between saying that a Muslim YMCA is really a terrorist command center and asking a set of questions about what should be built near the site where three thousand people were burned alive by terrorists. So why was this particular project under the microscope for so many? My own sense is that a large number of Americans were made uneasy by a combination of the deep pain they still felt around 9/11 and a sense of discomfort with Islam and Muslims. The carnival atmosphere around Cordoba House only increased their unease. No doubt the clear and present forces of prejudice of the Pamela Geller variety exploited the discomfort, but the reason it existed in the first place is because the movement I belong to had failed to replace the image of Muslims as terrorists with that of Muslims as neighbors. "The first job of a leader is to define reality," said Max DePree.[12] Those of us in interfaith work let other leaders define America as a nation that ought to be suspicious of one of its religious communities. That tragedy should be felt far beyond the community of people who pray toward Mecca.

I profile many people in this book, but the main character is the one I love the most—America. You will see my weakness for her at every turn. She is the nation I belong to, believe in, seek to build up. She is the ultimate composite character, a character with a complex and inspiring past, a character whose future will be determined by the many characters who call her home.

The strangest part of the Cordoba House debate for me was the idea of sacred ground. The people opposed to Cordoba House insisted that the blocks around Ground Zero constituted a holy area. Those who believed Cordoba House ought to stay in Lower Manhattan liked to point to the nearby strip joint and off-track betting parlor and say that that patch of land is just like any other. "Why can't you just move it ten or twenty blocks away?" a CNN anchor asked me on air at the height of the controversy. But that would still be sacred ground, I thought to myself. A hundred miles north, a thousand miles south, two thousand miles west—it's all holy.

I believe every inch of America is sacred, from sea to shining sea. I believe we make it holy by who we welcome and by how we relate to each other. Call it my Muslim eyes on the American project. "We made you different nations and tribes that you may come to know one another," says the Qur'an.[13] There is no better place on earth than America to enact that vision. It is part of the definition of our nation. "I say democracy is only of use there that it may pass on and come to its flower and fruits in manners, in the highest forms of interaction between men, and their beliefs—in religion, literature, colleges, and schools," sang Walt Whitman.[14]

Pluralism is not a birthright in America; it's a responsibility. Pluralism does not fall from the sky; it does not rise up from the ground. *People* have fought for pluralism. *People* have kept the promise. America is exceptional not because there is magic in our air but because there is fierce determination in our citizens. "The greatness of America lies not in being more enlightened than any other nation, but rather in her ability to repair her faults," Alexis de Tocqueville wrote. Every generation has to affirm and extend the American promise.

When I think of that promise, I think of the Christmas pageant at the Catholic school on the North Side of Chicago where my firstborn started his education. The school is an American rainbow: African, Polish, Mexican, Croatian, Indian—you name it, it's there. They are all gathered at the Christmas pageant. Ms. G's three-year-olds are standing on the rickety stage, gleefully parading about in their Santa hats. Zayd is talking to his friend Lisa, the Chinese girl with the white mom and the Pakistani aunt. I am cooing in the ear of our newborn baby when the signal comes and the class starts in on their assigned song. It's a little wobbly at first, but they catch the swing soon enough, and when they hit the chorus, I can't help myself—I start to sing along. I love this melody; I love the sight of my sweet kid among all these other sweet kids. I'm remembering the sheer awe I felt on my first hike in a redwood forest, the adrenaline pumping through my veins when I hailed my first taxi on the New York island. My sons will make their own memories on this blessed patch of Earth. One day they will realize just what it means that this land is their land, and that they share it with 310 million others.

When Zayd was a baby and woke up crying in the middle of the night, I would walk up and down our hallway singing him this song. It was a long time ago when I last sang it, maybe fifth grade, but the words came back easy, like they were written on my heart. There at the Christmas pageant, with my kids and my countrymen, I am bursting with pride and love. This is the American *shahada*—a declaration of faith to our nation, and to each other.

# PART I

# GROUND ZERO

The Muslims on the steps of New York City Hall had come to give Michael Bloomberg a piece of their mind. They were chanting slogans and waving signs. They wanted equal rights, what Jews and Christians had, what several cities in New Jersey already recognized, what having a 12 percent representation among the population justified, what a City Council resolution that passed by an overwhelming margin (impressive but nonbinding) warranted, what political organizing in a democratic system should rightfully win them. They wanted two Muslim holy days, Eid al Fitr and Eid al Adha, recognized as public school holidays.

The mayor was clear about his position, and he was not for turning. "If you close the schools for every single holiday, there won't be any school," Bloomberg curtly told the *New York Times*.[1]

The Muslims were not happy. Eid wasn't just *any* holiday, and they weren't just *any* community. They had rounded up their neighbors, they had formed a coalition with other community and religious groups, they had found their voice, and they were directing it at the mayor. "We really have confidence in the mayor's intelligence," said one of the coalition's leaders, Imam Talib Abdur-Rashid. "It's an election year," he added.[2]

Fatima Shama, then the mayor's senior adviser on education policy, remembers Bloomberg walking into the bullpen in City Hall that morning visibly frustrated. She overheard

3

him venting about it to other staffers, and she remembers thinking, "Actually, this is his fault.' A few weeks later, Fatima brought the issue up with him: "Mr. Mayor, you should know—they're out there *because* of you." Bloomberg, like any mayor, was accustomed to getting blamed for all sorts of problems, but he seemed positively baffled by having guilt assigned to him on this one. Fatima continued, "Remember those speeches you gave about every New Yorker having a voice? Remember how you assured Arab and Muslim New Yorkers not to be fearful because of the effects of 9/11? Well, they took you at your word."

Fatima was something of an anomaly at the senior levels of the mayor's office. Many of Bloomberg's staff were identified through national searches and had the same kind of Ivy League/private-sector success résumé he did. The vast majority were white. Fatima was from the Bronx and had degrees from Binghamton University (part of the State University of New York system) and Baruch College (part of the City College of New York system). After graduate school, she'd landed a job running a health-and-literacy project for the city. Her work was efficient and effective, and she got promoted multiple times in relatively short order, including into a position where she worked directly with the mayor. Then, when Fatima was barely in her thirties, Bloomberg appointed her New York City's commissioner for immigrant affairs, a result of both the connections she had with various ethnic and religious communities in the city and the trust the mayor had in her judgment.

Attractive, with olive skin, dark eyes, and long, curly hair, Fatima looks like the type of ethnically ambiguous woman New York City specializes in. One day, Bloomberg overheard her speaking Arabic to a Muslim delegation visiting City Hall. "But I thought you spoke Spanish," he said, a little surprised.

"I speak Spanish *and* Arabic," she said. "And Portuguese." Bloomberg looked even more confused, so Fatima added, by way of explanation, "My Brazilian mother raised me to be a good Arab housewife."

Fatima's father had fled the Arab-Israeli War in 1948 and gone to Brazil. He met and married a woman there, and the two immigrated to the United States in 1962. In his first years in America, Fatima's father worked as a peddler, finally scraping together enough money to start a store he named A & S Grocery. The *A* stood for *Ali* and the *S* for *Sons*. But Ali's sons—Fatima's brothers—didn't work in the store. They were busy with school, sports, and other seductions of American life. Fatima and her sisters were the ones who loaded soda bottles on grocery shelves and ran the cash register. "Why don't you call your store A & D Grocery?" she asked her father one day. "*D* for *daughter*," she said when he looked confused. Now he was even more confused. Palestinian Muslim men start stores with their sons, not their daughters. Everyone knows that. Why was this daughter always asking such questions?

Fatima was raised a Catholic in Palestinian culture with a sprinkling of Islam. She went to the same Catholic school as US Supreme Court Justice Sonya Sotomayor and attended Mass on Sunday. Her father didn't pray and didn't fast for Ramadan. The Islamic content of her house consisted of two oft-repeated ideas: *Allah maak* and *Haram*—"God be with you," and "Know what is forbidden."

In that tight-knit, largely Palestinian neighborhood, it felt like lots of things were forbidden, especially for girls. A group of families had chipped in twenty bucks each to purchase enough chairs for a few dozen Arab Muslim kids to sit in a basement and receive Islamic lessons from a severe-looking middle-aged woman every Saturday morning. On the handful of occasions Fatima attended, she remembers the lessons as long on lists of forbidden things. Pickles were on the list: they were shameful because of their shape. "I didn't understand why until years later," Fatima told me.

A lot of girls Fatima knew got married as teenagers. About the time she turned sixteen, she started getting visitors. It was not uncommon for her to come home from school and find, in the living room, a family with a grown son looking for a suitable match. Fatima would bring tea and stare ahead in stony silence. "I thought about faking a twitch to scare them off," she told me.

College offered the hope of freedom. Fatima had the grades; it was other hurdles she had to overcome. One afternoon, one of Fatima's aunts came to her home, sat on the same sofa the suitors and their families did, and loudly declared that girls going away to college is *haram*. Fatima's father listened politely and said he'd handle this. When his sister left, he turned to his daughter, who was bursting with opinions and intelligence, and said, "You go to college, but if you do anything to dishonor this family, you're in serious trouble."

On the first day of class, Fatima's sociology of religion professor read down the list of names. "Fatima Shama," he said, and Fatima raised her hand. He looked at her, smiled, and said, "*Salam alaykum.*" Fatima wanted to bury her head. She'd taken the class because she thought it would be an easy A. She had no interest in answering for a religion she felt no connection to. Actually, at that time in her life, she felt no connection to any religion. As a teenager, she'd gone to the Middle East and had been overwhelmed by the depth of suffering she saw in Palestinian refugee camps. She asked the priest at her church when she returned home why he never talked about the Middle East in his homilies. "No politics in church," the man said.

"I'm not asking you to talk about politics," Fatima said. "I just want you to talk about human suffering. Isn't that a central theme in Christianity?"

"No politics in church," the priest said, louder.

"I'm not coming back here," Fatima told her mother.

The head of the Newman Center, the Catholic students' organization, was in Fatima's sociology of religion class. So was the leader of Hillel, the Jewish student group. Both of them talked about their faiths with knowledge and pride. Faith guided their lives, faith illuminated their paths, faith inspired their actions. Fatima had always viewed faith as motions and mumbles you faked when other people were around. She put her nose to the ground at Islamic school when everyone else did; she knelt at Mass when everyone else got on their knees. But Fatima was fascinated by these other students in her class, these students who talked of the fullness and freedom that faith gave them. What was that about?

Because she was the only one with a Muslim-sounding name in class, people turned to her on questions about Islam. "I guess I could have said that I wasn't going to talk about it, that I wasn't really Muslim," she told me. "I could have even dropped the class. But the way these other two talked about their faiths, and because people looked at me when Islam came up, I decided I wanted to know something about this religion that other people wanted me to represent. So I started checking Islamic books out of the library and reading them late into the night."

One of the authors her professor recommended was Moroccan scholar Fatema Mernissi. Her work turned everything Fatima thought she knew about Islam upside down, especially when it came to gender relations. Mernissi wrote about Khadija, the Prophet's wife, presenting her as a successful, independent businesswoman so impressed by the work ethic and honesty of a younger man named Muhammad that she proposes marriage to him. As Muhammad goes through the experience of receiving revelation, preaching Islam, and being hated and threatened by the Quraysh tribe in Mecca, Khadija stands staunchly by his side, both supporting and guiding him. "I wanted to be like that—intelligent, independent, successful, but also a strong partner," Fatima told me.

Fatima met a Pakistani student on campus who taught her how to pray. She started fasting for Ramadan. She began to speak up in class, talking about the connection she felt to the Islam that she was reading about in the work of feminist scholars. As she deepened into her faith, she found her life growing fuller. As she accepted some of the restrictions within Islam, she felt freer. And as she moved toward making a career choice, her Muslim faith inspired her in the direction of public service.

Serving as the mayor's senior adviser on education and
being a Muslim during the time that Muslims were lobby-
ing City Hall for Eid to be a public holiday put Fatima in an
interesting position. Muslim leaders would contact her and
ask for meetings with City Hall brass. Fatima facilitated ac-
cess appropriately. These people were New Yorkers, and they
had every right to make their case to public officials. Fatima
also gave the mayor primers on Islam. She talked about the
Qur'an and the Prophet, the Five Pillars of Islam, the ritual
prayers, the centrality of mercy. She spoke about the signifi-
cance of Eid and the practice of *iftar,* the meal that ends the
daily fast during the month of Ramadan. She even convinced
Bloomberg to host an *iftar* dinner at Gracie Mansion, pointing out that the White House had been hosting such an event
since the 1990s. "He thought it was beautiful," Fatima told
me. "The form of the prayer, the sound of the *azaan*—he was
just blown away." He was particularly moved by the imam
who led the prayer at the *iftar,* a Muslim New Yorker from
Egypt whom Fatima recommended, a man named Feisal Abdul Rauf.

There seemed to be two modes for politicians when it came
to the Ground Zero Mosque debate in late summer of 2010:
attack or avoid. Those who opposed Cordoba House being
at 51 Park Place puffed up their chests, let out their roars, and
threw their spears every chance they got, which was pretty
frequently, because for several weeks straight, it was the first
question every journalist asked any politician. Carl Paladino
made it the centerpiece of his campaign for governor, running ads saying, "A mosque makes a mockery of those who
died there" and promising to use the power of eminent do-
main to stop "the monument to those who attacked us."[3] On
the other hand, every time the issue came up, political figures who thought New York City Muslims ought to be able
to pray where they wished and launch a center where they
wanted looked like they were seeking a rock to crawl under.
The standard bleat was, "They have the right to do it, even

though it may not be the right thing to do." This was effectively what President Obama said when he proclaimed he would not comment on the "wisdom" of the location.[4] Some cited the First Amendment guarantee of freedom of worship, or the fact that the courts would almost certainly allow Cordoba House to be built, but they did it so meekly, it sounded more like they were hiding behind the Constitution than defending it.

Bloomberg was virtually in a category by himself. Cordoba House became his signature cause that summer, a position that may well be the defining legacy of his third term as mayor of New York. Every political wind was against him: A Religion News Poll showed that, based on its proximity to Ground Zero, over 60 percent of Americans opposed Cordoba House. Eighty-five percent of Republicans, members of Bloomberg's political party, were against it. Even a majority of New Yorkers were opposed.[5]

Bloomberg didn't run away, he didn't hide, and he didn't compromise. Every chance he got he spoke up, with conviction and emotion. When his speechwriters presented him with language that he considered too weak, he wrote his own lines. When civic and religious leaders told him in private they thought he probably was right but didn't want to risk their reputations and appear with him in public on this issue, it just strengthened his resolve. Longtime friends went public with their disagreement with the mayor. The hate mail piled up at City Hall, some of it from former admirers saying that his stand on the issue had changed their opinion of him; if he ran for president, they would not support him. When the Anti-Defamation League stated that they were opposed to Cordoba House, the mayor didn't take a pass and say, "Well, they have a right to their opinion" or "I'm not going to comment on that."[6] He said the position was "totally out of character with [the ADL's] stated mission. I have no idea what possessed them to reach that conclusion." When New York governor David Patterson offered to give Cordoba House free state-owned land far away from Ground

Zero, Bloomberg—standing right next to Patterson at a press conference—openly disagreed with him. "Something about this issue just really hooked into him," Howard Rubenstein, a powerful business leader in New York and a friend of Bloomberg's, commented. "It deeply upset him."[7] Bloomberg told Daisy Khan (the face of the project in the media and Imam Feisal's wife) in private that Cordoba House should not move, no matter how hot the political fires burned or how good the offer to go elsewhere. He'd stand with them. The beating heart of New York City was on the line; the idea of America was at stake.

Bloomberg set out his case for American pluralism in two speeches he gave that August, right at the height of the media furor around Cordoba House. The first speech was delivered at the Statue of Liberty at the beginning of the month and the second at an *iftar* dinner the mayor hosted at Gracie Mansion toward the end of the month.[8] Part of the mayor's job in these speeches was being clear about who the enemy was, and who the enemy was not. "Islam did not attack the World Trade Center—al-Qaeda did," Bloomberg said at the *iftar*. Muslim New Yorkers were friends, neighbors, co-workers, just like everyone else. And just like everyone else in New York City on 9/11, Muslims were among those who suffered. "Let us not forget that Muslims were among those murdered on 9/11 and that our Muslim neighbors grieved with us as New Yorkers and as Americans," Bloomberg said. "We would betray our values—and who we are as New Yorkers and Americans—if we said 'no' to a mosque in Lower Manhattan."

Part of the mayor's job was to articulate a definition of America. He emphasized what our nation is not: "To implicate all of Islam for the actions of a few who twisted a great religion is unfair and un-American." He stated in no uncertain terms the core values of this country and presented New York City as the epitome of American pluralism: "Our doors are open to everyone—everyone with a dream and a willingness to work hard and play by the rules. New York City was built by immigrants and it is sustained by immigrants. . . . That's what makes New York special and different and strong."

For Bloomberg, it was precisely that pluralism that the 9/11 terrorists had attacked, and precisely that value that New York City and America had to now proudly embrace. "We would be untrue to the best part of ourselves—and who we are as New Yorkers and Americans—if we said 'no' to a mosque in Lower Manhattan," he said. "We would betray our values—and play into our enemies' hands—if we were to treat Muslims differently than anyone else. In fact, to cave to popular sentiment would be to hand a victory to the terrorists."

He supported Cordoba House not just because religious freedom was a cornerstone of American law but also because he expected the institution to make an important contribution to American life. "It is my hope that the mosque will help bring our city even closer together and help repudiate the false and repugnant idea that the attacks of 9/11 were in any way consistent with Islam. Muslims are as much a part of our city and our country as people of any other faith, and they are as welcome to worship in Lower Manhattan as any other group. . . . I expect the community center and mosque will add to the vitality of the neighborhood and the entire city."

Bloomberg offered special recognition to the parents of Mohammad Salman Hamdani, who had disappeared on the morning of 9/11. The family, like many families in New York City, frantically searched the city's morgues and hospitals for any sign of their son. In October 2001, they heard a knock on the door. It was two police officers, who asked a set of terse questions about Salman. They demanded the graduation picture they saw on the fridge, the one that showed Salman next to an Afghani classmate. Slowly, it dawned on the family: these police officers were basically accusing Salman of being involved in the 9/11 attacks. His Muslim faith and Pakistani background made him a prime suspect. There was a photo of Salman circulating through New York City Police Department offices with the caption "Hold and detain. Notify: major case squad."

It turns out that Salman was not one of the villains of 9/11, but one of the heroes. A certified emergency medical technician and a police cadet, Salman had seen the burning towers while he was traveling to work and gone to help. He died saving others. "Salman stood up when most people would have gone in the other direction," Bloomberg said of him.[9]

The mayor even defended the individual most other public figures, even those who supported Cordoba House, didn't want to talk about: Imam Feisal. During the furor around Cordoba House, all those world leaders Imam Feisal met through US State Department events and trips to Davos acted as if they'd never heard of him. Not Bloomberg. He quoted the speech Imam Feisal had made during a memorial service for slain *Wall Street Journal* reporter Daniel Pearl: "If to be a Jew means to say with all one's heart, mind, and soul 'Shma' Yisrael, Adonai Elohenu Adonai Ahad'—'Hear O Israel, the Lord our God, the Lord is One, not only today I am a Jew, I have always been one.' "[10] "In that spirit," Bloomberg continued, "let me declare that we in New York are Jews and Christians and Muslims, and we always have been. And above all that, we are Americans. . . . There is nowhere in the five boroughs of New York City that is off limits to any religion. By affirming that basic idea, we will honor America's values and we will keep New York the most open, diverse, tolerant and free city in the world."[11]

It was not the first time on these shores the forces of prejudice had sought to deny the contributions of a religious community, and it was not the first time someone had stood up to defeat those forces. There were battles between pluralism and prejudice long before this land was a nation, even before New York City had its name.

In the mid-seventeenth century, the Dutch director-general of what was then New Amsterdam, Peter Stuyvesant, banned Quaker prayer meetings. Quakers were viewed as dangerous rabble-rousers—"seducers of the people"—who posed a threat to his city. Stuyvesant ordered the public torturing of a twenty-three-year-old Quaker convert named Roger Hodgson and issued an ordinance that punished with imprisonment and a fine anyone found to be harboring Quakers.[12]

In most cities in most countries at most times, that's where the matter would have ended. Another religion banned, another community banished. But Edward Hart, the town clerk in a village just outside of New Amsterdam (now the site of Flushing, Queens, maybe the most religiously diverse neighborhood in the country) was determined that this land would be different. He gathered a group of his townsmen and drafted a petition taking a stand against what he viewed as blatant prejudice and in favor of a value he was willing to risk everything for: pluralism. Among the most remarkable things about the document is its breadth. The Flushing Remonstrance of 1657 did not speak only about Quakers, and it did not speak only of rights. There were lines about the dignity of all humans, coming as we do from the same single ancestor: "The law of love, peace and liberty in the states extending to Jews, Turks and Egyptians, as they are considered sons of Adam."

There was an exhortation that we see the good in all people, given that we are each of us animated by a divine source: "Whatsoever form, name or title hee appears in, whether Presbyterian, Independent, Baptist or Quaker, but shall be glad to see anything of God in any of them."

And there was the continual insistence that human beings of all faiths represent the greatest of God's gifts—love—and that for this reason, when a person or community comes in love, they ought to be received with grace: "Therefore if any of these said persons come in love unto us, we cannot in conscience lay violent hands upon them, but give them free egresse and regresse unto our Town, and houses."[13]

The Flushing Remonstrance is frequently cited as be-ing among the earliest articulations of religious freedom in America. But love is too central a theme for it to be under-stood as a narrowly legal document. In my view, the Flushing Remonstrance belongs more in the tradition of imagining America as a beloved community, a country that welcomes the contributions of all people, than as one outlining a code. Even more inspiring than the document's beautiful language and broad vision is this: none of the signers was a Quaker.

And while Edward Hart was a minor official, the stand he took for pluralism was mirrored by someone we lionize as one of our Founding Fathers. In 1790, President Washington heard a plea from Moses Seixas, of the Hebrew Congrega-tion of Newport, Rhode Island. Seixas was worried about the fate of Jews in the new nation. Would they be harassed and hated as they had been for so many centuries in Europe? Washington knew other religious communities had similar concerns. He chose the occasion of his response to Seixas to state plainly his vision for America:

> The Government of the United States . . . gives to bigotry no sanction, to persecution no assistance, requires only that they who live under its protection should demean themselves as good citizens. . . . May the children of the stock of Abraham who dwell in this land continue to merit and enjoy the good will of the other inhabitants—while every one shall sit in safety under his own vine and fig tree and there shall be none to make him afraid.[14]

Like the writers of the Flushing Remonstrance, Washing-ton is offering a vision of a national community, not simply articulating a legal doctrine: in America, people will have their identities respected, their freedoms protected, and their safety secured. They will be encouraged to cultivate good re-lationships with fellow Americans from other backgrounds, no matter the tensions and conflicts in the lands from which they came. And they will be invited—and expected—to contribute to the common good of their country. Respect, relationship, and commitment to the common good—those were Washington's three pillars of pluralism in a diverse democracy.

Washington came to his views through both principle and practical experience. As the leader of the Continental Army, the first truly national institution, Washington recognized he was going to need the contributions of all willing groups in America. The rampant anti-Catholic bigotry at that time was disrespectful to Catholic identity, a divisive force within the Continental Army, and a threat to the success of the American Revolution. Washington banned insults to Catholics like burning effigies of the pope, told his officers to make sure the contributions of Catholics were welcomed, and scolded those who disobeyed with words like these: "At such a juncture, and in such circumstances, to be insulting their Religion, is so monstrous, as not to be suffered or excused."[15]

It was the same in Washington's private life. When seeking a carpenter and a bricklayer for his Mount Vernon estate, he remarked, "If they are good workmen, they may be of Asia, Africa, or Europe. They may be Mohometans, Jews or Christians of any Sect, or they may be Atheists."[16] What mattered is what they could build.

A few months after 9/11, my father went to a banquet hosted by a Muslim activist organization. Somber prayers were offered for the victims of the attacks, and appropriate anger was directed at the terrorists. One of the hosts gave a passionate address about the coming threat to Muslims in America: how our rights were about to be trampled by the government in the name of security. The response, he told the fired-up crowd, should be a Muslim civil rights movement.

The chief guest at the dinner was the Reverend Jesse Jackson. Perhaps the Muslim speaker felt as if he was paying homage to the movement Jackson had helped lead. If so, what happened next must have come as something of a shock. Jackson opened his speech by saying there is no such thing as Muslim civil rights.

There is a well-honed sense of victimhood in some segments of the American Muslim community. You can see it in the e-mail newsletters of certain Muslim organizations. Every other story is an incident of a Muslim being wronged. Some Muslims have become expert in stringing such stories together, collecting them into a grand narrative of Muslim suffering stretching from Gaza to Green Bay. During the Ground Zero Mosque episode, I half-expected to see such newsletters linking the prejudice faced by American Muslims to the oppression of Palestinians, Iraqis, Afghans, and Chechens. Instead, something very different happened. American Muslims contextualized the Cordoba House events not in the narrative of global Muslim suffering, but in the arc of American minority groups that have experienced discrimination. The talk was not about Palestinians and Iraqis over there, it was about blacks and Jews right here. Muslims began studying the American experience from the perspective of minorities that had been marginalized. They expected to find parallels to their own suffering. What they did not expect was a lesson in what it means to be American.

America has not been a promise to all its people. "We didn't land on Plymouth Rock," Malcolm X said. "Plymouth Rock landed on us." Whatever the faiths of the workmen who came to Mount Vernon, they laid their bricks next to Washington's slaves. We are a nation whose creed speaks of welcoming all communities and whose practice has too often crushed them. But, to borrow from Maya Angelou, the dust was determined to rise, and generous enough to carry the rest of us with. People who knew the whip of the slave master in Alabama, the business end of the police baton on the South Side of Chicago, people who could easily have called our nation a lie, chose instead to believe America was a broken promise, and gave their bodies and their blood to fix it.

As Langston Hughes wrote, even though "America never was America to me," he was still committed to making the promise of this nation real, declaring one line later in his poem, "America will be."[17]

That night at the Muslim activist banquet, Jesse Jackson wanted to make sure his audience left with a full understanding of the meaning of the civil rights movement. The marches, the sit-ins, the braving of fire hoses and attack dogs, had not been about safeguarding the rights of one community. The purpose was to expand and secure a framework that protected all communities. "We weren't fighting for black civil rights," Jackson told his audience. "We were fighting for *your* civil rights. You have a choice right now: you can talk about an America where *your* people don't get sent to the back of the bus, or you can talk about an America where *no one* gets sent to the back of the bus."

I could sense the emotion in my dad's voice when he called to tell me about the event. He paused for a long time, collecting his thoughts, and then said, "We owe our presence in this country to that movement."

It was a movement not for the African American Dream but, in the words of Jesse Jackson's mentor, Martin Luther King Jr., for "the American Dream, the dream of men of all races, creeds, national backgrounds, living together as brothers." It was not only a movement that helped pass legislation dismantling racist policies in the domestic realm but also a movement whose spirit changed immigration laws as well, ushering in the Immigration Act of 1965, legislation that allowed people like those gathered at that Muslim banquet to come to America. King had a vision of a nation where all communities participated in the privilege and responsibility of pluralism, a vision that included religious identity as readily as race: "One of the first things we notice about this dream is an amazing universalism. It does not say some men, it says all men. It does not say all white men, but it says all men which includes black men. It doesn't say all Protestants, but it says all men which includes Catholics. It doesn't say all Gentiles, it says all men which includes Jews."[18]

Registering your story in the narrative of American discrimination offers opportunities for commiseration, but more importantly, it gives your community a dramatically expanded set of responsibilities. You quickly learn that other American communities used their moments of suffering to work for a nation where no one suffers. You quickly realize that other people's struggles have secured your rights. It begins to dawn on you that you have a responsibility to use the moment when the spotlight shines on you to secure the rights of others. "Whoever degrades another degrades me," wrote Walt Whitman.[19] That is the heart of the American spirit.

It was a lesson I learned from John Tateishi, executive director of the Japanese American Citizens League. One of John's earliest memories was being released from an internment camp. His father held him by the shoulders and said, "Son, do not forget this moment, and do not let America forget it. This country is too good for what it did to us."

On the morning of 9/11, John was heading south on I-5 out of Seattle, driving to an early meeting. He was casually turning the radio dial when he caught the news of the first plane hitting the tower. He turned the volume up and listened as the second plane hit, the towers collapsed, and threats directed at Muslims started to pour in. He turned his car around and called his assistant. "Cancel my meetings for the rest of the week," he said. "And start calling our regional directors. Tell them to cancel their meetings. The focus of our organization has just become about the protection of American Muslims." When I asked him why he did that, he told me how grateful he was for the people who stood up for Japanese Americans during World War II. Had there been more, he believed, the internment camps would not have happened. When it was his turn to protect another community, it was his responsibility to take it. The most American thing you can do is stand up for someone else.

We hosted an intern at Interfaith Youth Core during the Ground Zero Mosque crisis who embodied that ethic. His name was Nick, he was from nearby DePaul University, and he had the task of tracking the hurricane of media relating to Muslims during that time. He spent hours every day reading the hundreds of articles and blog posts on the slings and arrows suffered by Muslims, and compiling reports on the trends, highlights, and points of concern. One day, he wrote an article of his own. It was about Tyler Clementi, the Rutgers University student who committed suicide after his sexual encounter with a man was streamed live.[20] Nick wrote that he understood Tyler Clementi because, as a gay man, he had planned his own suicide many times. He described it in detail: the note he would write, the pills he would swallow, the look on his grandmother's face when she found his body.[21]

I had been so consumed by the rampant Islamophobia of 2010 that I had completely missed the bigotry others were suffering around that same time. Yes, we Muslims faced an ugly strain of intolerance, but nothing like what the lesbian, gay, bisexual, and transgender community had suffered— torture in the Bronx, bullying so severe it led to multiple suicides. It amazed me that a member of that group was spending his time sticking up for Muslims. Why would Nick volunteer for an organization advocating for religious pluralism? For Nick, the reason was simple: if he wanted his community to be free and safe in America, he had to work for an America where everybody was free and safe.

Talking to Nick about his essay, I realized just how many people had stood up for Muslims during the Ground Zero Mosque crisis. Our allies included Evangelical Christian ministers, hip-hop moguls, Jewish comedians, gay atheists— the list goes on. I couldn't help but wonder, would we Muslims take risks to stand up for them? Would we support Nick when he suffered antigay bullying? You cannot ask from others what you are unwilling to give.

———

My interview with Fatima was at City Hall. I wanted to speak with her in her work environment, and I wanted to see the famous chair facing two computer screens in the bullpen where the mayor sat. I didn't realize that City Hall was so close to Ground Zero and thus to 51 Park Place, the site of Cordoba House. I started out in that direction and was soon lost in the spaghetti bowl of streets in Lower Manhattan—Park Row, Park Place, Chambers, Beekman, Broadway. The longer I walked, the more I tasted the flavors of New York's urban masala: A guy wearing a cowboy hat standing outside a doorway saying, "Dominican hair salon, Dominican hair salon." Groups of suburban high school students dressed in canary-yellow T-shirts on a field trip to the city. Bankers and secretaries catching discreet smokes fifteen feet away from office buildings. On Broadway, a few blocks north at Astor Place, a small group of Hare Krishnas beating their drums, chanting their chants, and serving free food underneath a Kmart sign.

The sculpture of the large black cube at the Astor Place subway stop brought to mind the Ka'aba in Mecca. I thought about the Emma Lazarus poem inscribed on the Statue of Liberty: "Give me your tired, your poor / Your huddled masses yearning to breathe free." The openness of the invitation from the Muslim poet Rumi would fit alongside perfectly: "Come, come, whoever you are . . . Ours is not a caravan of despair."[22]

My conversation with Fatima had been inspiring. I viewed her as part of a new turn in the immigrant thread of the American Muslim experience. Being Muslim wasn't a default mode for her, something she had blindly absorbed from her parents and continued practicing robotically. Islam was a proactive choice, one that she had made in a world of other options. It was a religious identity nurtured by being around people of other faiths, one deeply connected to serving the diverse community that surrounded her. Dr. Umar Abd-

Allah of the Nawawi Foundation, perhaps the most broadly respected Muslim scholar in America today, speaks of the importance of indigenizing Islam in America.[23] The manner in which Fatima carried out her work as an American Muslim in a senior post in the Bloomberg administration illustrated that indigenizing.

Even though she had personal sympathies with the Muslims campaigning for Eid as a public school holiday, Shama ultimately advised the mayor against it. She simply could not justify disrupting school for over a million students, teachers, and staff so that a fraction of those could celebrate a religious holiday. Rather, she advised, Muslims would be free to take those days off to celebrate with their families, schools should accommodate appropriately, and everyone else should show up to learn. I asked her why she chose that course. "My job is to advise the mayor to take policy positions that will help this whole city thrive," she explained to me. "When the whole city thrives, individual communities thrive."

She was equally clear in her support for Cordoba House. It was an American institution founded by Muslims that would serve the city. Lower Manhattan would benefit enormously from a swimming pool, a public art space, and a beautiful auditorium. She told the mayor that it was exactly the kind of place she wanted to bring her children, a place where they could say their prayers as Muslims and then engage in arts projects with Jews, Christians, and humanists. That was exactly the kind of institution Bloomberg wanted in his city. And then he shared why the issue was so personal to him.

It turns out that Michael Bloomberg, one of the richest people in America, a man who had won an unprecedented third term in one of the most visible and influential positions in American politics, a Master of the Masters of the Universe, had a childhood memory of prejudice that still stung. He remembered a time when his family, because they were Jewish, could not purchase a home outright in the Boston suburb of Medford. They had to ask their lawyer—a Christian—to buy it and sell it back to them. It was a personal thread in the fabric of religious prejudice in America. Some people experience bigotry and respond, "I'm going to help build a world where that never happens to *my people* again." Michael Bloomberg experienced it and decided, "I'm going to help build a world where that never happens to *anyone* again."[24]

A year after the Summer of Islamophobia, Fatima and I were on a panel together talking about the Muslim American experience. Fatima made it a point to emphasize that she had worked just as hard on the antigay bigotry of the fall of 2010 as she had on the anti-Muslim bigotry of that summer. Making sure gays felt safe in New York City's boroughs was just as Muslim a thing to do as making sure Muslims feel safe.

Listening to Fatima speak of the work she did as an American Muslim on behalf of the LGBT community, I thought of a famous saying of the Prophet Muhammad: "No one of you truly believes until he wants for his brother what he wants for himself."

It is an ethic central to Islam. It is an ethic, in a hundred languages and in every conceivable form of prayer, that has built America.

# THE MUSLIM MENACE

In October 1995, just months after graduating from law school, Suhail Khan moved home to San Jose. One day, taking the local paper out of its wrapper from the driveway of his parents' home, he found himself stunned by the story splashed across the front page. Longtime US congressman Norman Mineta had announced that he was resigning his seat in thirty days. Mineta, a Democrat, had lost his powerful position as chair of the Transportation Committee in the Republican revolution of 1994, and had decided that taking a job as a corporate lobbyist for Lockheed Martin would be more fruitful than being in the minority.[1] The article listed a number of prominent Bay Area Democrats who would likely compete for the seat. Toward the end, somewhat offhandedly, it suggested that there might be a Republican candidate as well—Tom Campbell.

That name rang a bell for Suhail. Campbell was a professor at Stanford Law School and a state senator. Suhail knew the name from California state Republican circles. Campbell had a reputation as a man guided by principles, not partisan ideology or personal ambition. Among other things, Suhail had always respected that he didn't take political action committee money.

Suhail, who had attended law school at the University of Iowa, was hoping to turn his familiarity with that all-important early caucus state into a position with a Republican presidential candidate. He'd been having promising conversations with staff in the Bob Dole campaign, but the possibility of being involved in a race in his home district intrigued him. He called Stanford Law School to see if he could get through to Campbell. After being transferred around for a while, he finally heard Campbell's voice on the other end of the line. Suhail explained that he'd read the *Mercury News* article and that he'd like to find out more about Campbell's campaign. Campbell said that he'd read the same article and was intrigued by the possibility himself.

"You mean you haven't announced that you're running yet?" Suhail asked, a little surprised.

"Mineta's announcement shocked everyone. I haven't even had time to decide whether I want to run, let alone announce it to a newspaper," Campbell explained. He had spent much of the morning trying to get through to his wife, who was in Russia at the time. He took down Suhail's number and said he'd get back to him if he chose to get into the race. Suhail had been around politics long enough to know not to wait by the phone.

Born in Colorado and raised in Northern California by Indian Muslim immigrant parents, Suhail traced his interest in politics back to both his parents' influence and to a chance moment in American television. As a kid, he happened to be watching *Schoolhouse Rock* on the day the animated educational show for children had a civics lesson. "I'm just a bill," sang a rolled-up piece of paper on the steps of Capitol Hill, in Washington, DC. Suhail remembers the cartoon well—the American flag waving over the portico of the Capitol, the description of American government and democracy, the whole song the rolled-up piece of paper sang. And he remembers thinking to himself, "I'm going to be a part of that someday."

Suhail traces his inspiration for joining the Republican Party to an even more unlikely source: the University of California at Berkeley. Suhail enrolled there in 1987, when he was seventeen. "There were a bunch of policies—local and campus ones, mostly—that I found well-intentioned but ineffective," he said. "Rent control was one; affirmative action was another. On one level, they made sense to me, but in the final analysis, I thought they did more harm than good. And in some cases, they were just downright contradictory. For example, at the same time there were these huge pro–affirmative action protests at Berkeley, there was a cap on the number of Chinese students there. No doubt blacks have experienced terrible discrimination in America, but so have Chinese Americans. It seemed illogical to aggressively recruit one group based on the idea of redressing past wrongs while limiting another that had also experienced discrimination."

Suhail laughed when he talked about having joined the Berkeley College Republicans, aware of how oxymoronic the phrase sounds. And indeed, it was the smallest college Republican group at any university in California. Not long after joining, he was given a leadership position. By the time he left Berkeley, Suhail had grown the Berkeley College Republicans into the largest such campus group in the state. His success on campus led to Suhail being offered a staff position in the California Republican Party, where he worked on the George H. W. Bush campaign in 1988. When I asked him his core reason for being a Republican, Suhail answered simply that America should rely on the entrepreneurship and goodness of its citizens, not on the well-intentioned but ineffective policies of government agencies, to be a great society. It wasn't just a political idea, he pointed out, but a religious one as well. Islam emphasizes humankind's agency and virtue. We ought to have a society that frees up those qualities.

It was one of the connections he felt with Tom Campbell. "He's a very devout Catholic, although he never wore it on his sleeve," Suhail told me. "He went to Mass several times a week and took part in all kinds of Bible studies. But more importantly, he was the kind of guy who wanted to live a life that lived up to the ideals of his faith. He wanted to look himself in the mirror every morning and feel like he was doing that." Suhail had gone to Catholic school in the Bay

Area, attended both Catholic Mass and *jumma* prayers at the mosque each week, and knew well the resonances between the traditions. Neither Campbell's Catholic faith nor Suhail's Muslim faith played much of a role in the campaign. Suhail couldn't remember anyone in the California Republican Party ever asking him about Islam, much less his faith being a problem.

Campbell won the special election big and decided to take one person from his campaign with him to DC: Suhail. When he arrived, Suhail was the only Muslim congressional staffer on the Hill. He would pray in the corners of empty rooms and offices, sometimes even in stairwells or hallways. Campbell discovered him doing so one day and told him, "You can always pray in my office." When a second Muslim arrived on Capitol Hill—a staffer for Congressman Jesse Jackson Jr., a Democrat from the South Side of Chicago—the two of them would pray together in Campbell's office.

Many congressional offices look like shrines to the current occupant. Signed pictures of the official with baseball players, rock stars, celebrities of all sorts are stuffed together on the walls as a way to exude an aura of importance, as if the office itself isn't enough. Campbell had none of those. "The guy was just focused on his job," Suhail said. "It made him very hard to buy gifts for."

When Mother Teresa came to DC, Suhail felt like he had his chance: "She embodied Campbell's vision of selfless service, rooted in the Catholic faith." Suhail bought a picture of her, waited in line to get it signed, and offered it to Campbell. It was Suhail's way of thanking the man who had given him his shot in national politics, and for expressing respect for what Campbell held most dear. Campbell put it up in his office. One day, Suhail came into the office and saw something taped to the picture. It was a verse from Surah Miriam, a passage from the Qur'an on the holiness of the Virgin Mary. It was Campbell's way of thanking Suhail.

Suhail was overjoyed at having a place besides stairwells and hallways in which to make his daily prayers, but *jumma* on Fridays was another matter altogether. It wasn't a problem to get the time off from work—Campbell had stated that he would not hold staff meetings on Fridays at midday. But Campbell's office was too small to host a Muslim *khutba,* or sermon, or anything close to a congregation. Suhail and his Muslim friend on the Hill started carpooling to a mosque in downtown DC. Soon, other Muslim federal employees heard about the Muslim caravan and asked to join in. Two people became eight, then ten, then twelve. Suhail was happy for the growing community of Muslims, but as soon as the numbers hit about twenty, they decided the caravan was becoming too cumbersome.

Suhail suggested finding a regular place in the Capitol building itself. "I lived a block away from it at the time," he told me. "It's this towering, beautiful, imposing structure, made of cast iron. It's a symbol of American democracy. It was important to me that building stood for the principles it was built on—equality and freedom. I thought, 'What better way for the Capitol to feel alive than to have federal employees of a religious minority praying here, openly and proudly.'" They approached the House chaplain, who immediately suggested the House chapel for their Friday prayers. The only problem was the chapel had wooden pews bolted to the ground, meaning there wasn't enough space for Muslims to perform their prayers. They were going to have to find someplace else.

One of the quaint relics of American politics is that the Speaker of the House controls the rooms on the House side of the Capitol. Suhail knew it was going to be a long, hard road to convince the Speaker to assign a room for weekly Muslim prayers. Space is short in the Capitol, the request list for it is long, and there are a lot of powerful people on that list. Suhail strategized about the coalition he would build, thinking through the various heavies he would bring in to lean on the Speaker and the number of meetings it might take. He told his Muslim friends that he doubted they'd get the space weekly. The likelihood was a monthly *jumma* on Capitol Hill, and Suhail estimated it could take up to a year to finalize.

Somewhat randomly, Suhail found himself standing next to the Speaker at a reception and decided, "Why not introduce the idea now?" "Mr. Speaker," he began and, in a crowded room, to the soundtrack of clinking cocktail glasses, he described the growing number of Muslim federal employees and the ins and outs of Muslim prayer practice. The Speaker nodded and listened. "How many people are we talking, total?" he asked.

"About thirty," Suhail replied.

"What kind of room setup do you need?" the Speaker asked.

Suhail explained how Muslims pray on carpets, facing toward Mecca, and assured the Speaker that his group would take full responsibility for moving the tables and chairs around as needed, and put them back when they left. "I'd like to schedule a time to speak with you about this more fully," he said. And then he quickly added, "I'd like to bring in some others as well."

The Speaker waved him off, replying that such a step wouldn't be necessary. Suhail and his fellow Muslims would have their weekly prayer space. Moreover, the Speaker would arrange for the building staff to set up the room properly. "As long as I'm Speaker, you'll have space for fifty every Friday afternoon," he assured Suhail.

Suhail remembers a journalist from Turkey visiting Washington, DC, on assignment, and coming across his group of American Muslim federal employees holding *jumma* prayers on Capitol Hill. "The guy couldn't pick his jaw up off the floor," Suhail said. "I mean, he was just stunned. At that time in Turkey, which is a majority Muslim country, you couldn't show any sort of religiosity in public buildings, not even wear a headscarf if you were a Muslim woman who covered. They were scared of the majority religion, let alone minority communities. The fact that the United States—a country with a Christian majority—was giving a group of Muslims official space to pray in one of the symbols of its democracy was simply too much for him." Suhail paused and then continued, "That's America, that's what this country is about, that's what the world should see when they see us."

The journalist asked him who had made the decision to give the Muslims the space to pray. Suhail told him: the Speaker of the House, a man just after the vice president in the succession to the presidency, a Republican from Georgia who had engineered his party's takeover of the House of Representatives after forty years of rule by Democrats, a former history professor named Newt Gingrich.

I was an undergraduate at the University of Illinois during the years Suhail Khan was looking for space to pray in the Capitol, running with a politically active and progressive crowd. The name Newt Gingrich was generally preceded by a series of expletives and followed by the time and place of the next protest. We called Gingrich's Contract with America the "Contract *on* America" and made all kinds of off-color jokes when Gingrich resigned as Speaker of the House because of a sexual relationship with an aide in his office. In his television appearances back in the mid-1990s, Gingrich had struck me as mean not just in policies but also in personality—always wearing a scowl, generally pointing a finger (literally and figuratively), frequently looking like he wanted to take a swing at whoever was interviewing him, and maybe some of the audience members as well. But Gingrich never struck me as *religious mean*. Guys like Jerry Falwell and Pat Robertson were religious mean. They didn't want to just punch you, they wanted to smite you. Gingrich had never been particularly connected with that crowd. His issues were fiscal—balanced budgets, lower taxes, welfare reform—and he spoke about them primarily in terms of national strength, not Christian values.

Frankly, I'm not proud of my stridency back then. My college roommate actively avoided me, leaving our dorm room early and coming back late, because he knew I could barely take two breaths without emitting a volley of invective on the fundamental brokenness of American politics. Gin-

grich, more often than not, was the centerpiece of those ti-
rades. A few years later, my views having moderated and my
networks expanded, I was having dinner with a friend who
worked at the American Enterprise Institute (a conservative
think tank in Washington, DC) who casually mentioned that
Gingrich was based there. I'd forgotten about him by then,
figuring that he'd gathered whatever scraps of dignity he
could salvage after his much-publicized affair and resigna-
tion and retreated back to Georgia to teach history at some
college way out yonder. "Oh, no, he's still around," my friend
said, a wry smile playing on his face. Apparently, Gingrich
had gone through something of a transformation, one cen-
tered on religion. He'd recently married Callista Bistek and
was showing serious interest in her Catholic faith. He was
also playing a hugely influential role in conservative circles,
advising Republican politicians, raising money for conservative causes, and continuing to be an indefatigable idea
factory. But Gingrich, as my friend pointed out, had always
seen himself as a front man, and it was unlikely that he was
going to stay behind the scenes forever. "You'll be hearing
from him again" was my friend's guess.

For a conservative politician seeking to reintroduce himself to the broader American public, the Cordoba House
controversy was like a fastball down the middle of the plate.
An anti-Muslim movement had been growing across America in the years after 9/11. Anti-Muslim websites like Pamela
Geller's *Atlas Shrugs* were receiving hundreds of thousands
of hits a month.[2] Brigitte Gabriel's ACT! for America, whose
purpose is to root out Muslim influence, boasts five hundred
chapters around the country.[3] Anti-Muslim authors like Robert Spencer had several books on Amazon's Top 25 list on Islam and were regularly invited to be guests on respected talk
shows. The core message of the industry of Islamophobia was
simple and clear: Muslims are preparing a takeover of America because their religion requires them to. There is no such
thing as a good Muslim. There is no such thing as moderate
Islam. They are not like us. They are against us. *We have to
stop them now.*

Their talking points co opted key Muslim concepts in an attempt to masquerade as educated. To them, *dawa* did not mean education about Islam; it meant domination. Sharia was not simply Muslim law, a system with strong analogues in Judaism and Catholicism; it meant the public stoning of women in summer clothing—better stop it before it comes to your Oklahoma town! *Taqiyya* was not a minor Islamic practice allowing Muslims to dissimulate when someone seeks them harm; it was a core feature of the faith that requires Muslims to lie about their true objectives. The only Muslim groups with similar interpretations of such Islamic concepts were extremists. And so a peculiar partnership emerged: on matters of Islamic doctrine, Pamela Geller agreed with Osama bin Laden.

The industry of Islamophobia had slogans and campaigns, speakers and authors, policy papers and websites, organizations and networks. It was a civil-society movement waiting for its moment and its champion. They had been building the wave for years, their efforts crested with the Cordoba House controversy, and Newt Gingrich was only too happy to ride it.

Gingrich was everywhere during those weeks, providing red-meat sound bites on television, writing about the controversy for newspapers, making it part of his policy speeches at think tanks. The political webzine *Talking Points Memo* called Gingrich "the nation's spokesperson for Islamophobia."[4] The issue was perfect for the former Speaker of the House—it allowed him to play populist and professor, to show off his PhD in European history and his heartland patriotism. There he was on Sean Hannity's show saying in an August 2010 interview, "This is purely and simply an anti-American act of triumphalism on the part of a radical Islamist who is going to go around the world and say, 'See, the Americans are so dumb that after we destroy two of their greatest buildings, they allow us to build a mosque near there, and that tells how weak and how ignorant Americans [are]." On *Fox & Friends* that same month, he compared Cordoba House's proximity to Ground Zero to Nazis putting up a sign next to a Holocaust memorial. In the *Washington Post,* Gingrich offered a history lesson: "Cordoba House is a deliberately insulting term. It refers to Cordoba, Spain—the capital of Muslim conquerors who symbolized their victory over the Christian Spaniards by transforming a church there into the world's third-largest mosque complex." Each of these lines was quoted hundreds if not thousands of times on websites, in speeches, at rallies. Gingrich was both supplying ammunition for the movement against Muslims in America and leading the charge. After a decade in the political wilderness, Newt Gingrich was out front again.

Ever the wily politician, Gingrich accurately predicted that the Cordoba House issue was likely to disappear as quickly as it had arrived, a phenomena produced by a 24/7 cable news machine seeking a controversy in the notoriously slow-news weeks of late summer. The anti-Muslim sentiment would continue to simmer, but would require a new hook to stay in the spotlight. It didn't take Gingrich long to find it. In a policy speech at the American Enterprise Institute, he spoke darkly of the infiltration of sharia law into the United States. Gingrich claimed that any activity that facilitated sharia's advance should be stopped. He chose to single out the growing industry of sharia financing: "Teaching about sharia financing is dangerous," Gingrich claimed, "because it is the first step toward the normalization of sharia, and I believe sharia is a mortal threat to the survival of freedom in the United States and in the world as we know it. I think it's that straightforward and that real."[5]

Like his statements on Cordoba House, Gingrich's comments about sharia were quoted repeatedly by the press and became a rallying point for the anti-Muslim movement across America. They were widely credited with the movement to ban sharia law in Oklahoma, a referendum that passed with 70 percent of the vote in a state where sharia law was never proposed and Muslims make up less than 1 percent of the population. Knowing that he'd struck political gold, Gingrich continued his campaign. At the Values

Voter Summit, he received a standing ovation when he called for "a federal law that says sharia law cannot be recognized by any court in the United States." To commemorate the ninth anniversary of 9/11, Gingrich wrote a piece in which he warned of the presence of stealth radical Islamists: "In addition to the violent Radical Islamists who would use force to destroy America, there are stealth Radical Islamists who use our political system and our commitment to free speech and liberty to undermine our democracy through infiltration, intimidation, and propaganda. Both the violent Radical Islamists and the stealth Radical Islamists represent a mortal threat to the American system of Constitutional Law and political freedom."[6]

The great scholar of religion Reinhold Niebuhr once wrote that the most useful lens through which to view the intersection of religion with politics in American history is irony. Irony allows you to look at situations that might be considered tragic and find the comedy, to view instances that might initially cause you to laugh out loud and pause to locate the deeper meaning. Irony can be defined as the "apparently fortuitous incongruities in life which are discovered, upon closer examination, to be not merely fortuitous." It is at work when "virtue becomes vice through some hidden defect in the virtue." And, above all, Niebuhr emphasized, *"The ironic situation is distinguished from a pathetic one by the fact that the person involved bears in it some responsibility for it."*[7]

When it comes to Gingrich and irony, it's hard to know where to start. There are ample examples, both personal and political. As he was lecturing salt-of-the-earth Midwesterners on fiscal prudence, he maintained a half-million-dollar credit line at the jewelry store Tiffany's. The extramarital affair that drove Gingrich from office in the late 1990s was in full (ahem) swing at the same time he was spearheading impeachment proceedings against Bill Clinton for the president's liaison with Monica Lewinsky. He publicly railed against the mortgage giant Freddie Mac for its role in the mortgage crisis but happily accepted over $1.5 million in consulting fees from it.[8] But the ironies layered in Gingrich's dealings with Islam take the cake, not just for what they say about the former Speaker, but about what they illustrate with respect to the intersection of religion and politics in America in the early days of the twenty-first century.

As his conversation with Suhail Khan suggest, Newt Gingrich was a friend to Muslims long before he was a friend to Muslim haters. Not only did he provide Muslims a space to pray inside the US Capitol in the 1990s, in the early 2000s Gingrich attended meetings of the Islamic Free Market Institute, whose mission was to promote education about sharia-compliant banking and finance among Americans, supporting a practice that he called a mortal threat to freedom a few years later. But back then, Gingrich saw a political opportunity in the growing Muslim population. According to someone present at one of the meetings, Gingrich "was very positive, very supportive. His whole attitude was that Muslims are part of the American fabric and that Muslim Americans should be Republicans." Gingrich's overtures were well received by some segments of the American Muslim community. In 2007, a group called Muslims for America wrote in its newsletter that Gingrich should be nominated for president, stating that "unlike other politicians, Gingrich doesn't see us at war with Islam."[9]

In his 2006 *New York Times* best seller *Rediscovering God in America,* Newt Gingrich wrote, "It is a testament to the genius of the Founding Fathers that they designed a practical form of government that allows religious groups the freedom to express their strong religious beliefs in the public square— a constitutional framework that avoids inter-religious conflict and discrimination."[10] He referenced the philosopher Michael Novak's insight that reverence for God and fidelity to core principles had given rise to both remarkable religious diversity and inspiring religious tolerance in America. He quoted Alexis de Tocqueville's observation that religion in

America played a key role in supporting civic institutions. And he spoke proudly of the American tradition of according respect to all religions.

This all makes Gingrich sound like the man Suhail Khan came to Washington to work for, Tom Campbell. Both were Republicans who viewed religious pluralism as a central element of American greatness, and who found ways to extend that respect in both their personal and professional lives. It was thanks to Campbell that Suhail had a space for his private prayers in the Capitol, and thanks to Gingrich that Muslim federal employees had a space for their congregational prayers. Suhail viewed these gestures as entirely consistent with Republican Party values—equal freedom for all groups and the welcoming of faith in the public square. In addition to party affiliation and agreement on the role faith should play in America, Gingrich and Campbell have, as of 2009, something else in common: a church.

Newt Gingrich can be seen most Sundays sitting in a pew awaiting the noon mass at the Basilica of the National Shrine of the Immaculate Conception, a Catholic church in northeast Washington, DC, watching his wife Callista sing in the choir. When they are on the road, whether they are in Des Moines or Costa Rica, he and Callista find a local Catholic church to attend. Gingrich has written about "the beautiful experience" of listening to "Amazing Grace" being sung in Chinese at Mass in Beijing, of "marveling . . . at the historic truth of the church" on his first visit to St. Peter's Basilica, of the comfort he takes in being surrounded by two millennia of church history and teaching. He describes Pope Benedict XVI's 2008 visit to Washington, DC, as a turning point for him. Gingrich attended the private vespers service Benedict presided over with the US Conference of American Bishops and found himself awed by the pope's very presence: "Catching a glimpse of Pope Benedict that day, I was struck by the happiness and peacefulness he exuded. The joyful and radiating presence of the Holy Father." It was the event, Gingrich said, that moved him to formally convert to the Catholic faith.[11]

The Catholic leader Gingrich speaks most passionately about is Pope John Paul II, calling him "one of the most consequential figures of our lifetime." He and Callista cohosted a film about John Paul II's life and took it on tour around the country. The message of the film focuses on the impact of faith in the world, using the example of John Paul II's role in liberating Poland and defeating communism through the power of freedom through faith. It's a message that Gingrich believes America needs now more than ever. In Gingrich's comparison, contemporary America, like Communist Poland, has banned school prayer, knocks crosses off public spaces, and considers it more acceptable to be an atheist than a Christian.[12]

Gingrich rarely used his Catholic faith as a reason to bash Muslims. The Catholic Church, at least since the Second Vatican Council in the 1960s, has been quite clear on its respect for other world religions, especially Islam and Judaism. In fact, the man Gingrich called "one of the most consequential figures of our lifetime" was also the man who built powerful bridges between the Catholic Church and Muslim communities around the world. When Pope John Paul II went to Morocco in 1985, he was the first Holy Father to visit an officially Islamic country. In his address to thousands of young Muslims in the stadium in Casablanca, he said, "We believe in the same God, the one God, the living God."[13] Six years later, John Paul II was the first pope to visit an Islamic house of worship, the Umayyad mosque in Syria, where he paused to pray before a memorial to John the Baptist, an event televised across much of the Muslim world. There were symbolic events like two World Peace Prayer Days held at Assisi, and there were scholarly bridges, like the ties between Catholic scholars at the Vatican and Muslim scholars at Al Azhar. In other words, it is Catholic theology to build bridges with Muslims.

---

And it is a fact of American history that for much of our nation's past, the Catholic Church was viewed as a seditious force and the Catholic masses were referred to as "the Catholic Menace." As a former professor of history, Gingrich knows as well as anyone that we live in a unique time in America, a time when he can speak openly about the beauty he finds in Catholic ritual and the admiration he has for Catholic leaders, and feel confident that his faith will not only be accepted but will also be viewed as a political asset. In past eras, such statements would have earned Gingrich the reputation of being a stealth agent for the Catholic hierarchy, a tool of foreign elements, of using America's freedom of speech and open political system to threaten that very system. "The deepest bias in the history of the American people" is how historian Arthur Schlesinger Jr. referred to our nation's history of anti-Catholic prejudice. In short, once Gingrich would have been accused of the very crimes he accuses Muslims of now.

Had Gingrich been walking a village green in any city on the Eastern Seaboard during colonial times, he might have come across a "Pope's Day" celebration where the effigy of the Holy Father was burned, children sang anti-Catholic songs, and adults toasted the overthrow of "the Beast" prophesied by the Book of Revelation. Gingrich could not have pursued a political career in those times, because in many of the colonies, Catholics were forbidden from holding public office, even from serving on juries. In fact, had Gingrich been searching for a place to celebrate Mass in Lower Manhattan through most of the eighteenth century, he would have come up empty. In the same area where Gingrich registered his opposition to Cordoba House, priests were subject to arrest and Catholics were effectively barred from practicing their faith. It wasn't until the late 1700s that the first Catholic parish, St. Peter's, was established, and even then Manhattan residents demanded that the church be built outside of the city limits. There were concerns that foreign money from the enemies of New York was involved, and indeed King Charles III, of Catholic Spain, made a $1,000 contribution, a royal sum two centuries ago. On Christmas Eve 1806, in one of the many demonstrations outside of St. Peter's, the building was surrounded by people enraged by the service of "popish superstition" occurring inside, otherwise known as Christmas Mass. Dozens of people were injured and one died in the riot.

In the nineteenth century, as Catholic immigration to America swelled, the anti-Catholic movement grew and got more organized. The best-selling books, the high-profile speakers, and the growing civil-society organizations like the American and Foreign Christian Union had a clear and compelling message: Catholicism was a foreign and seditious force on American soil whose purpose was to convert the masses to an evil, lustful religion. America is by nature free and open; Catholicism is inherently authoritarian and dominating. If allowed to grow, it would replace the American government with the Catholic hierarchy and plant the flag of the pope at the White House. The Catholic strategy of domination was to spread through its institutions—its schools, its churches, its hospitals—each one a Trojan horse carrying the hateful faith inside.

There were slogans and campaigns, speakers and authors, organizations and networks, policy papers and that era's version of websites—tracts. Had Gingrich been browsing in a bookstore at that time, he would have seen a best seller called *The Awful Disclosures of Maria Monk* on prominent display. The book chronicled the life of a Protestant teenage girl captured by Roman Catholic clergy and forced to do their bidding. The confessional was a place where priests raped nuns, the convent a place where the children of these unions were buried after they were baptized. The mother superior explained to poor Maria, "Their little souls would thank those who kill their bodies, if they had it in their power."[14] *Awful Disclosures,* along with *Uncle Tom's Cabin,* was one of the best-selling books of antebellum culture.

Lyman Beecher, one of the most respected Evangelical figures of his era, was also one of the most prominent speakers on the anti-Catholic circuit. On August 10, 1834, Beecher gave a series of sermons in Boston churches, claiming that "the principles of this corrupt church are adverse to our free institutions" and using as a prime example the Ursuline Convent in nearby Charlestown. Had Gingrich been in Charlestown twenty-four hours later, he would have watched the crowds burn the convent to the ground.

By the mid-nineteenth century, a political party emerged to ride the wave of anti-Catholic sentiment that the civil-society movement had expertly cultivated. It was commonly called the Know Nothings because its members, when asked what they knew about the party's workings, would say, "I know nothing." In 1854, this party so dominated American politics that it elected seventy-five people to Congress, and legislatures in several states were composed almost entirely of Know Nothing politicians. Politicians who were running unopposed on the ballot would find themselves defeated by write-in candidates affiliated with the Know Nothings. Abraham Lincoln observed, "Our progress in degeneracy appears to me to be pretty rapid. As a nation we began by declaring that 'all men are created equal.' We now practically read it 'all men are created equal, except negroes.' When the Know Nothings get control, it will read, 'all men are created equal, except negroes, and foreigners, and Catholics.' "[15]

The Know Nothings sought to prevent Catholics from establishing their institutions and influence in America. If they had won, it wouldn't simply be Catholics who suffered. The 573 Catholic hospitals in the United States, which treat over 85 million patients a year, might not exist. Nor would the 231 Catholic colleges and the 7,000 Catholic elementary and secondary schools, which educate over 2 million students a year, a third of whom are members of racial and ethnic minorities. Catholic Charities USA provides social services for over 10 million people a year. Almost all of these institutions— hospitals, schools, colleges, social-service agencies—serve people beyond the Catholic community. In fact, that is part of how they understand their mission: Catholics for the common good. It is a system of service so large and impressive that, without it, American civil society would literally be unrecognizable.

The Know Nothing Party, like the headlines around Cordoba House, faded as suddenly as it arrived. But anti-Catholic prejudice remained an American hallmark well into the twentieth century. There were the hateful hoods of the Ku Klux Klan and the bigotry that helped defeat a Catholic candidate for president, Al Smith, in 1928. Most famously, there was the movement against another presidential candidate who happened to be Catholic and faced a highly organized opposition largely from Evangelical Protestants in America: John F. Kennedy. I have no doubt that Gingrich studied that election closely. But unlike his fellow Republican Michael Bloomberg, Gingrich didn't take away a deep sympathy for those who suffer religious prejudice. Instead, he learned the tactics of the perpetrators.[16]

# THE EVANGELICAL SHIFT

In May 1959, George Gallup released a survey showing that over one-fourth of Americans said they would not vote for a Catholic for president. Gallup's research showed that John F. Kennedy led Richard Nixon by 57 percent to 43 percent among likely voters when religion was not called to their attention.[1] The fear in the Kennedy camp was that those numbers would change markedly if faith was brought to the forefront.

The Kennedy strategy was to distance him from the Catholic hierarchy as much as possible. He met in private settings with Protestant leaders who expressed concern about his faith, and submitted himself to their soft inquisition. For every possible issue in which there might be a concern about how Catholicism impacted public policies, Kennedy erected a wall between his faith and his politics: Were Catholics required to attend Catholic schools? No, he and his brothers had attended other schools. Would a Catholic politician hire only Catholic staff and appoint only Catholics to powerful positions? No, hiring and appointments would be based on merit—just look at his Senate office. What about federal funds for Catholic schools? The Supreme Court had ruled such funding unconstitutional, and Kennedy agreed with that. Would he appoint an ambassador to the Vatican? He would not.[2]

Kennedy hoped that these private meetings would quiet the Catholic questions. They didn't. During the campaign,

Kennedy's faith kept coming up, requiring him to do interviews and give major speeches on the subject. He told *Look* magazine in February 1959, "Whatever one's religion in private life may be, for the officeholder, nothing takes precedence over his oath to uphold the Constitution in all parts—including the First Amendment and the strict separation of Church and State."[3] In April 1960, he told the American Association of Newspaper Editors, "I am not the Catholic candidate for President. I am the Democratic Party's candidate for President who happens to be Catholic. I do not speak for the Catholic Church on issues of public policy, and no one in that Church speaks for me."[4] And, in one of the most memorable speeches made by a presidential candidate in recent American history, he told the Greater Houston Ministerial Association in September 1960, with just a few weeks to go until the election, "I believe in an America where the separation of church and state is absolute; where no Catholic prelate would tell the President—should he be Catholic—how to act. . . . I want a chief executive whose public acts . . . and whose fulfillment of his Presidential office [are] not limited or conditioned by *any* religious oath, ritual or obligation."[5]

As Kennedy did his best to keep religion out of the election of 1960, a group of Evangelical Protestants were doing their best to keep the issue on the front burner. In April 1960, the National Association of Evangelicals passed a resolution that stated that "due to the political-religious nature of the Roman Catholic Church we doubt that a Roman Catholic president could or would resist fully the pressures of the ecclesiastical hierarchy."[6] Evangelical publications offered the specter of a nation under the thumb of the Church. "A Catholic President: How Free from Church Control?" was the cover story in the May 1960 issue of the NAE's flagship magazine. A tract published by the organization titled *Shall America Bow to the Pope of Rome?* included a picture of the US envoy to the Vatican, Myron Taylor, bowing before the pontiff. Wherever Catholics were a majority, these Evangelicals claimed, the church hierarchy put policies in place that marginalized other communities. *Crimes of Intolerance: The Slaughter of Protestants in Mexico and the Fate of Protestants in Columbia* and *The Truth about the Protestant Situation in Spain* were two popular tracts along these lines.[7] The Catholic hierarchy, the claim went, had similar designs on America. Selective quotes from Catholic leaders were trotted out for proof: a 1948 statement of the US Conference of Catholic Bishops that called the separation of church and state a "shibboleth of doctrinaire secularism," a quote from Pope Leo XIII from 1885 that called for Catholics to "penetrate, wherever possible" into circles of influence in their nations.[8]

One of the leading forces among Evangelicals seeking to keep Kennedy from the White House was Billy Graham, the reigning king of the community, perhaps the most influential American Protestant of the twentieth century. Graham carried on a correspondence with Nixon, pleading with him to raise the issue of Kennedy's Catholicism "at this uncertain hour of history." He invited Nixon to make a public visit to his home in North Carolina, believing that it would both tip that state in his favor and focus the spotlight on the religion issue. Graham also emphasized that he himself was playing a direct role in influencing the election of 1960. He had encouraged the Southern Baptist denomination to pass a resolution that was effectively a denouncement of Kennedy and an endorsement of Nixon. He had also sent a letter to the 2 million American families on his mailing list encouraging them to "organize their Sunday school classes and churches to get out the vote."[9]

In the summer of 1960, Graham brought a group of American Evangelicals together at a conference in Europe to set a strategy to defeat Kennedy. It was a moment of inspiration for Norman Vincent Peale, one of the nation's most prominent religious figures and one of Nixon's former pastors. Peale decided to make Graham's mission his own, and to continue to galvanize Evangelical forces in America against the Kennedy candidacy. On September 7, 1960, at the Mayflower Hotel, in Washington, DC, Peale held a gathering that amounted to a larger, higher-profile follow-up to the Graham meeting. "Our freedom, our religious freedom, is at stake if we elect a member of the Roman Catholic order as president of the United States," Peale told the conference of 150 people representing a broad spectrum of American Evangelical Christianity. The conference manifesto stated that the "actions and policies of the Catholic Church have given Protestants legitimate grounds for concern about having a Catholic in the White House." Each participant received a fact sheet on what made the Catholic Church so dangerous. Among the charges were the following:

> The Roman Catholic church is both a religion and a political force whose doctrine is ultimately incompatible with the American ideals of freedom, equality and democracy;

> Wherever Catholicism is the majority religion, it dominates other groups and faiths, effectively making them second class citizens;

> The Catholic Church demands total obedience and gives explicit guidance on a comprehensive range of belief and behavior;

> If conflicts arise between the conscience of the individual believer and the doctrine of the church, these are always resolved in favor of the Church. Individuals who persist in their own independent thought are excommunicated;

> The Catholic Church, through both its religious figures and elected officials, has a history of exerting its influence on public policy for its own benefit, including procuring funds for its own schools and hospitals.[10]

The Reverend Harold Ockenga, pastor of the Park Street Church, the flagship of New England evangelicalism—located at the corner of Boston Common, where Lyman Beecher had stirred the Protestant masses to violence a century earlier—gave one of the opening keynotes. "If we want to know what will happen if Roman Catholic America ensues, we must understand the official teaching of universal Roman Catholicism," he declared.[11] The purpose of the Catholic hierarchy was to become the state, he continued, to use the instruments of government to convert every soul and to program the thoughts and actions of every citizen. And Catholics, he warned, were closer to their goals than most Americans thought. Their numbers were growing in America at an alarming rate. Once they achieved some combination of critical mass plus political influence, well, the best Protestants could hope for was to be tolerated. The election of John F. Kennedy could well be the final straw.

What of the fact that Kennedy had repeated over and over again that he believed unambiguously in the separation of church and state, that the church would neither influence nor speak for him on matters of public policy, that his record of fourteen years in Congress betrayed no evidence of preferential treatment for the views of the Catholic Church? According to Ockenga, none of this mattered. The Catholics had a doctrine called mental reservation that allowed them to lie in order to advance their faith.[12]

Ironically, Protestant politicians were all over the map on the various issues that American Evangelicals put before Kennedy. For much of the presidential campaign of 1960, Nixon refused to say whether he would appoint an ambassador to the Vatican. Moreover, Roosevelt, Truman, and Eisenhower—all Protestants—each did appoint such an envoy. And on the central issue, whether religion should influence politics in America, the Evangelicals organizing against Kennedy were far guiltier than the Catholic candidate. They were, with seemingly no sense of irony, using the power and platform provided by their religious offices to force a presidential candidate to say he would grant no power to religion.[13]

"John is such a poor Catholic," his wife, Jacqueline, once remarked about him. His aide and confidante Theodore Sorensen claims that he never remembers Kennedy talking about religion in any depth. But for the anti-Catholic forces of the mid-twentieth century, the question wasn't about how Catholic Kennedy was; it was about the thirst for dominance of the Catholic hierarchy, the inherent totalitarian code of the tradition itself.

Replace "Catholic" with "Muslim" and "church hierarchy" with "sharia law" and, fifty years later, the pattern is repeating itself. Like the anti-Catholic movement of the nineteenth and twentieth centuries, the central argument of the forces of Islamophobia is that the very nature of Islam is in conflict with American values, especially freedom of religion and the separation of church and state. The problem is not with individual believers; the problem is with the belief system, which requires its adherents to adopt its policy of domination. Their secret weapons are overpopulation, conversion, and acquiring the mechanisms of political influence. The best evidence for this is in how that religion is wrecking other countries—Latin American nations, in the case of Catholicism; the Middle East, in the case of Islam. And the danger is not only in developing nations; ample evidence exists of the domination of the Catholic hierarchy or sharia law in Europe. When speaking of such dangers, above all else, be dire. Highlight America's imminent decline. Underscore the need to wake up and recognize that the barbarians are at the gate: "Our American culture is at stake," Peale said of the prospect of a Catholic in the White House in 1960. "I won't say it won't survive, but it won't be what it was."[14] "Nobody in our secular elites is prepared to stand up and defend Western civilization against the routine steady erosion," Gingrich told his audience at the American Enterprise Institute.[15] In today's parlance, Kennedy was part of a stealth jihad meant to replace the American Constitution with sharia law launch a *dawa* offensive on the American population, and he was practicing *taqiyya* in order to get elected.

At one of the early debates between the 2012 Republican presidential candidates, the question was raised about whether any of these candidates would allow Muslims to serve in their administrations. Not without an explicit declaration of their loyalty to the United States, said Herman Cain, a declaration that he would not require of either Jews or Christians. This was Gingrich's moment, and he seized it. He told the story of a Pakistani-American Muslim who built a car bomb that luckily failed to go off in Times Square (without, incidentally, mentioning the Muslim street vendor who notified the police about the suspicious vehicle) and continued, "Now, I just want to go out on a limb here. I'm in favor of saying to people, if you're not prepared to be loyal to the United States, you will not serve in my administration, period."[16]

As he said it, I had two thoughts. The first was whether Gingrich the historian, the recently converted Catholic, the man who had helped Muslims find a place to pray in the Capitol, who had gone to meetings about sharia financing with the goal of wooing Muslims into the Republican fold, who had written eloquently on America's first principle of religious tolerance, was giving any thought to what a past Catholic candidate for president had experienced on account of his faith. The second was which group did Gingrich seek to appeal to with that statement? That's when it occurred to me: the very community that opposed Kennedy's candidacy based on his Catholicism was attracted to Gingrich's presidential aspirations because of the Speaker's recent conversion. A mere fifty years separated the two campaigns. It was one of the most remarkable shifts in the religious and political landscapes in American history, a shift that Newt Gingrich was going to take full advantage of.

"I began to realize that what happens with Evangelical

Protestants and with Catholics is this strong sense of . . .
assault . . . they are under siege from radical Islamicists,"
Gingrich told the *Los Angeles Times*.[17] After the spectacular
fall, Gingrich's subsequent political rise can be attributed in
no small part to the popularity he has built with Evangelicals. Gingrich has somehow managed to make his personal
sins work for him politically with this group, tearfully asking
forgiveness of God, country, and Evangelical kingmakers
like James Dobson. Many Evangelicals have been moved by
these acts of contrition, and impressed by Gingrich's conversion to their policy issues. In 2009, Gingrich institutionalized
this support, launching Renewing American Leadership, an
organization whose mission is "to preserve America's Judeo-
Christian heritage by defending and promoting the four pillars of American civilization: faith, family, freedom, and free
enterprise." The board and staff involve highly influential
Evangelicals like David Barton, a phony historian who likes
to portray America's founders as the fathers of a Christian
nation, and Jim Garlow, who spearheaded the campaign to
prevent same-sex marriage in California. Gingrich's central
role in the Cordoba House affair and the anti-sharia movement have proved quite useful to Renewing American Leadership, helping the organization raise millions of dollars and
gather names and addresses that can easily be repurposed as
a list of supporters for a presidential campaign.[18]

Gingrich seems to enjoy the company of Evangelicals in
Iowa best of all. In 2010 and 2011, he visited the state often
and typically had meetings with pastors on his schedule. "I
think he's just excellent," gushed Pastor Brad Sherman of the
Solid Rock Christian Church in Coralville. So did the majority leader of Iowa's state House of Representatives—whose
company all the prospective 2012 GOP candidates appeared
to enjoy—and who gave his endorsement to Gingrich.[19] Gingrich played a key role in the unprecedented campaign to
recall three Iowa state Supreme Court justices who approved
same-sex marriage, offering "strategic advice" and arranging
for about $200,000 in seed money. Iowa is, of course, the

state that holds the first caucus in the presidential race, giving it outsize political influence. Sixty percent of Iowa Republican caucus-goers describe themselves as Evangelicals, and a large number seem quite taken by Gingrich's faith, even though it is not the same as theirs.

The Catholic Church is not Gingrich's first religion, and Callista is not his first wife. The former Speaker is on his third in both departments. Raised a Lutheran, he left that church to become a Southern Baptist (an Evangelical denomination) when he lived in the South, and he left the Southern Baptist tradition for his current Catholic faith around the time he started making noises about running for president. But if anything raises the eyebrows of Evangelicals about Gingrich's candidacy, it is his number of marriages, not his number of conversions. Richard Land, for one, remarked that Gingrich has "one ex-spouse too many for most Evangelicals."[20] Land, president of the Southern Baptist Convention's Ethics and Religious Liberty Commission, frequently represents Evangelicals in the media. That he appears more concerned about Gingrich leaving his second wife than his second church (the one he served as a senior officer, no less) is further evidence of just how much religious attitudes and interfaith relations have changed in the past half-century in America.

*Sharia* translates as "the path to a watering place." In a religious context, the term refers to various abstract values like the importance of life, religion, and education as well as more practical matters dealing with prayer times and funeral rites. In other words, it's the ways of believing, behaving, and belonging that makes Muslims Muslim. The key sources of sharia are the Qur'an and the example of the Prophet Muhammad. Throughout the course of Islamic history, various Muslim scholars applied these sources to real-life situations in different ways, a process of judicial interpretation known as *fiqh*. Plainly speaking, there is not a single sharia, just as there is not a single way of being Muslim. In Muslim-speak, there are a variety of schools of *fiqh*. But in any version of sharia, criminal codes—meaning punishment for destructive or deviant acts—are a very small part. When the term *sharia* comes up in an American court, it almost always has to do with personal matters like marriage and divorce, probating wills, and resolving money disputes—the very same matters other religious communities expect American courts to consider.[21]

This is one of the reasons many American Jews have found themselves alarmed by the anti-sharia movement. In fact, a number of Jewish groups have sent letters to state legislatures considering sharia bans, urging them to reject such laws. As an article on the Jewish Telegraphic Agency's website by Ron Kampeas stated, "If the state legislative initiatives targeting sharia are successful, they would gut a central tenet of American Jewish religious communal life: The ability under US law to resolve differences according to *halacha,* or Jewish religious law."[22]

The evidence that Muslims are poised to impose a draconian version of sharia in America boils down to a single court case in New Jersey. A Muslim woman sought a restraining order against her husband, stating that he was forcing her to have sex with him. The man claimed that sharia law allowed him to do so. The trial judge agreed with the man and did not issue the restraining order. The appellate court overturned the trial judge's ruling, stating that US criminal law trumped any other body of law. Abed Awad, a New Jersey–based attorney and an expert on sharia, wrote, "The appellate ruling is consistent with Islamic law, which prohibits spousal abuse, including nonconsensual sexual relations."[23]

While the material used to justify the sharia scare is thin, there are instances when other religious laws have been cited to cover up clear and heinous crimes. Joanne Mueller was surprised when her seven-year-old seemed upset that Father John Geoghan was coming over to visit. He was a popular, playful priest, and she was a single mother of four boys, over-joyed that a man wearing the safety of a collar would come to take her kids out for ice cream or to play in the park. Father Geoghan even did bedtimes, and he didn't mind giving the boys baths. "He was our friend," she said. Something strange was happening with her son that evening, though. He didn't seem happy about the news that Geoghan was on his way. He was silent for a while, and then he started to sob. "What is going on?" Mueller wondered, thoroughly confused. Fi-nally, her son said, still wailing, that he didn't want Father "touching my wee-wee." Mueller simply stared at her seven-year-old in disbelief. She summoned her youngest son, five years old, and told him that Geoghan was coming over. He broke down into tears as well. She called for her two older boys. When she mentioned the priest's name, they stood next to their two sobbing brothers, stiff and speechless, and then they started to cry as well. Then the oldest took the respon-sibility to speak the words of their shame aloud: "Father said we couldn't talk about it and tell you, never to tell you, be-cause it was a confessional."[24]

It was raining and cold outside, and Father Geoghan was about to arrive. Mueller put coats on the boys and raced them out the door, driving them to their parish, St. Mary's in Melrose, where she asked to see Reverend Paul Miceli, a parish priest who knew both the family and Geoghan. Miceli was overwhelmed by the story. Mueller later testified that he said, "He will never be a priest again. It will never happen again." That was 1973. Geoghan would continue his sexual abuse of boys while wearing a Roman Catholic collar for the next twenty-three years. His principal targets were the boys of poor, overwhelmed, single mothers, women who felt blessed to have a father figure in the lives of their sons. It was an arc of abuse that lasted nearly thirty years and that likely included somewhere between five hundred and a thou-sand victims.

Church officials knew from the very early days. Parents like Joanne Mueller told them in emotional personal meetings. Family members too intimidated or ashamed to confront a church official in person wrote letters telling their stories. At least once, another priest caught Father Geoghan in the act. One victim tells the story of a priest walking in on Father Geoghan as he was performing oral sex on the victim in the upper rooms of a rectory. "Jack, we told you not to do this up here," the victim recalled the priest saying. Geoghan was not only moved time and time again, he was also given plum assignments, including a summer-long retreat in Rome with $2,000 of spending money.[25]

Writer (and liberal Catholic) Anna Quindlen said of the clergy child-molestation scandal that "the bishops . . . were allowed to make their own laws."[26] It is not just a figure of speech. In May 1993, as the ironically named Cardinal Law, who had been head of the Archdiocese of Boston since the early 1980s, was trying to discern a way forward through the mounting allegations of priest sexual abuse, he asked a group of eminent experts in the field of child sexual abuse to advise him. They came for lunch at his palatial Italian Renaissance residence in the Brighton area of Boston. Carol Newberger, a child psychologist, was very clear about the proper procedure: report any cases to the civil authorities, remove any accused priest immediately, and keep them as far away from children as possible, because the likelihood of repeated behavior is extremely high. After studying the cases, she and the other experts told Cardinal Law in no uncertain terms that he and the Catholic Church had mishandled the situation, paving the path to further abuse rather than preventing it.

The more they talked, the more they felt they were not getting through. According to Newberger, the cardinal sat stone faced and silent most of the time. When he finally spoke, it was not to voice his sympathies for the victims and their families or to declare his anger at the priests who would abuse their collars; it was to say that the Catholic Church had its own ways of dealing with such matters. In situations like these, the cardinal stated, canon law had to be considered.

The words fell like a hammer on the gathering of child psychologists. "Whatever we had just told him didn't seem to be registering," Newberger later said. "Canon law was irrelevant to us. Children were being abused. Sexual predators were being protected. Canon law should have nothing to do with it. But they were determined to keep this problem, and their response to it, within their culture."[27]

For people familiar with the anti-Catholic tropes of previous eras, this sounds like the worst of the Evangelical predictions coming to fruition: It is priests abusing their privilege to prey on others. It is the sexual abuse suffered by Maria Monk (who, incidentally, was a fictitious figure), except forced on poor prepubescent boys instead of a novice nun. It is the Catholic hierarchy being party to the ugliest evil.

And though there has been a responsible movement seeking appropriate reform so that such a scandal never occurs again, there has been no widespread panic about Catholic influence in America. There is no legislation pending in twenty-plus states to make canon law illegal. Newt Gingrich, when he was talking about his Catholic faith on the campaign trail, was not asked if he would allow canon law to protect pedophile priests were he to win the White House. Senator John Kerry, a Boston Catholic and the Democratic Party's nominee for president in 2004, was not accused of being the tip of the spear for the Catholic hierarchy's American takeover. Nor were Vice President Joe Biden or Nancy Pelosi, the Speaker of the House from 2008 to 2010. Nor, to my knowledge, were any of the six Catholics who serve as US Supreme Court justices. Catholics have gained significant influence in American society, even while some of the most respected members in their fold have been guilty of abusing the power of their collars in the most reprehensible ways. The American public has made very little connection between the two.

In fact, Evangelicals have swung in the opposite direction, a dynamic illustrated by their support for both Newt Gingrich and his fellow Catholic in the 2012 Republican primary, US senator Rick Santorum.[28] It was Santorum who

received the plurality of the Evangelical vote in Iowa and Santorum who won states like Alabama and Mississippi, where
approximately eight out of ten Republican primary voters are
Evangelicals. Santorum is a life-long Catholic and very publicly associated with the conservative wing of the Church.
His opposition not only to abortion and same-sex marriage
but also to contraception has been a hallmark of his political
career. Many Evangelicals cheered when Santorum accused
one of their fellow Protestants, Barack Obama, of having a
"phony theology" not based on the Bible. The Evangelical
mega-leader Franklin Graham, son of the famous Billy, said
on morning television that he couldn't say for sure if Obama
(again, his fellow Protestant) was Christian but felt entirely
certain of Santorum's good standing in the faith.[29] And
when Santorum declared that he wanted to "throw up" when
he read Kennedy's Houston speech, in which JFK stated
his belief in the absolute separation of church and state—a
speech that Kennedy gave to assuage the concerns that mid-
twentieth-century Evangelicals had about too much Catholic influence in the White House—early-twenty-first-century
Evangelicals supported Santorum in the face of the public
outcry.[30] Fifty years ago, Evangelicals organized an all-out
effort to prevent a nominal Catholic from winning the White
House because they were afraid he would take his marching
orders from the Pope. In the 2012 Republican primary, Evangelicals organized an all-out effort in support of a Catholic
candidate who promised to do precisely that.

In the early 2000s, as the clerical-abuse scandal was unfold-
ing, Robert Putnam was undertaking an ambitious statistical
survey of Americans' attitudes toward the various religious
groups in our nation. The results showed that Catholics were
among the most favorably viewed. Muslims, on the other
hand, were at the bottom of the likeability barrel.

Looking at this data, it occurred to me that the two big
media stories about religion during those years were Muslim
extremism and clerical molestation. Barely a week went by

without a story of a suicide bombing or an accused priest on the evening news. Both Muslim extremism and clerical molestation involved only the smallest fraction of the larger body. Why did the first taint an entire religious community while the second didn't? Why were ordinary Muslims (who were far more likely than any other religious community to be killed by Muslim extremists) suspected of actually being terrorists, while most Catholics were viewed as victims of predatory priests? Based on his research, Putnam believes that the central reason is that most Americans, over the course of the past two generations, have had the occasion to meet and become friends with Catholics. In that process, they've learned to admire things about the Catholic faith, and they've learned that fears of Catholic domination are somewhere between unfounded and ridiculous. Most Americans are far more likely to associate the Catholic faith with their Catholic friends than with pedophile priests. Unfortunately, the same is not true for Muslims. Not enough people report a positive relationship with a Muslim or appreciative knowledge of Islam to counter the negative representations they see on television.

It's hard to overstate the role of Evangelicals in all of this. For many generations, they were the chief perpetrators of anti-Catholic prejudice. Now they seem to have turned that animus toward Muslims, using some of the same archetypes that they once applied to Catholics—a religion bent on domination, a tradition inherently opposed to freedom, a seditious force within our nation. I've heard people draw a straight line between the anti-Catholicism of the past and the Islamophobia of the present, essentially saying that the Evangelical impulse is to hate *someone,* the only question is who. I find that cynical. Seeing only the consistency of prejudice clouds a more important story when it comes to Evangelicals—the story of change.

The fact is, when it comes to relations with Catholics, Evangelicals have traveled a long way in a very short time. And the Catholic issue isn't the only area in which Evangelicals have changed. On everything from attitudes toward AIDS to protecting the environment, from race relations to relations with Jews, there is marked positive progress. Evangelicals constitute 40 percent of our nation, too huge a group to write off or to get wrong, and one with cultural power even greater than their numbers suggest. Simply put, when Evangelicals change, America changes.

The Evangelical shift around Muslims is starting to happen. Some of the most powerful allies Muslims had during the Ground Zero Mosque debate were Evangelicals. Jim Wallis, of the Christian social-justice organization Sojourners, was on television regularly sparring with the anti-Muslim crowd, saying that his mother always told him to stand up to bullies on the playground and that's all these people were. Gabe Lyons, founder of the Christian learning community Q, invited Imam Feisal to share the stage with him for a plenary presentation at the 2011 edition of the Q conference, one of the most important gatherings in the Evangelical movement. But for me, the most striking story of an Evangelical supporting Muslims was of a pastor with a strong Southern accent and a megachurch outside of Dallas, a guy who knows something about prejudice and change.

Growing up as an Evangelical Christian in East Texas in the 1960s, Bob Roberts remembers guest preachers climbing into the pulpit of his father's Southern Baptist church and talking about the pope as "the Great Whore of Babylon," the false prophet referred to in the Book of Revelations destined to lead a false church bent on world domination. The books he checked out of the church library said much the same: Catholics are not Christian. They believe in things like penance and good works, they have a different Bible, they pray to Mary. *They do not know Jesus.*

"That's what you were taught?" I asked.

"And it's what I taught others," he responded. "I started preaching as a teenager. I took the idea of spreading the one true faith very seriously, and I was good at it. I'd get up in pulpits and tell people about the false prophet, the false church, the false prayer. It was all part of teaching right and wrong, convincing them to stay on the one true path, the path of conservative Evangelical Protestant Christianity."

In 1985, at age twenty-seven, Bob started his own church in a Dallas suburb called Keller. But what he really wanted to do was be a missionary, to take his gift for bringing people to the one true path to those wandering astray in the darkest corners of the darkest places in the world. Each time he went before the International Missionary Board of the Southern Baptist Convention and presented his skills and wishes, he was turned down. He did not take this in stride. He would pray, "God, I am your faithful servant and a heckuva preacher. I can do you lots of good in the world. Why won't you let me help you?" Finally, an opportunity presented itself.

"There was a guy at my church, a Vietnam vet who had been shot down three times in the war," Bob said. "He'd become a medical doctor and done quite well for himself. He had some contacts in North Vietnam, and he suggested we go there, spread the gospel and such." If there was one group Bob feared more than Catholics, it was Vietnamese Communists. Growing up, he'd watched the guys he looked up to, who laughed and played baseball and bought Cokes for the kids, go off to Vietnam and come back in stony silence, broken, or not come home at all. "I remember sitting in my dad's car with the windows down as he went in the funeral home to visit a family whose son had been killed in the war," Bob said. "I could hear the wailing outside." Bob was scared, but he was also excited. Who better to convert than your former enemies? It was a sweet sort of revenge to bring those who once sought to kill American Christians back to the straight path. You could call it a holy victory. At that time, in 1995, Vietnam still severely restricted religion, so Bob couldn't go formally as a missionary; he had to get a humanitarian visa.

Bob got to be friends with the Vietnamese authorities. The rule was no preaching, but Bob didn't want to just go sightseeing and have lunches with dignitaries. His church back home was involved in all kinds of community projects. Some of the Vietnamese officials knew about those, and they proposed he try to launch some in Vietnam, starting with building schools and clinics. It became something that galvanized Bob's whole church community. Delegations started going to Vietnam regularly—sometimes twenty delegations a year—building schools and clinics. Wherever they went, there was always another group of people who seemed to be there first, who had already built schools and clinics and were happy to work with the Northwood church group on more projects: Catholics. When Bob asked one why they were involved like this, he answered, "Well, we believe in works."

There was only one functioning Protestant church in North Vietnam at the time. Bob remembers driving the roads around Hanoi and being surprised to see old, run-down Catholic churches, a vestige of French colonialism. He remembers thinking to himself, "If the Vietnamese people are ever going to come to know Christianity, it's probably going to be through those churches." And then he caught himself: Catholics aren't Christian, right?

Bob remembers seeing an old Vietnamese Catholic priest coming out of one of the churches wearing a collar. Just being openly identified with a religion was taking a great risk. The Communist government had the authority to arrest religious leaders, an authority it exercised frequently. On that fact alone, Bob admired this man's faith commitment.

The man was nervous when Bob approached him but seemed calmed when Bob said he was a Christian. Bob told him that he was part of a group that was bringing Americans to Vietnam to build schools and clinics. The Catholic priest nodded, happy to learn that Americans knew something of Vietnam other than the war. He noted that much of his work was building schools and clinics as well; it was part of the Catholic faith. Bob asked if there was anything he could do for the priest. The man said he needed Bibles.

This was a perfect missionary opportunity. This agent of

the Great Whore of Babylon was relying on Bob, a follower of the one true path, to bring him the Scriptures. One of the greatest cleavages between Catholics and Protestants in American history was over which Bible to use. The Catholic Bible contains several books the Protestant Bible does not. Riots broke out in several American cities in the nineteenth century because Protestants believed Catholics were going to use their Bible in public schools. Bob could have easily sent this man thousands of copies of the Protestant Bible and taken pride in bringing the true Gospel to a false follower in Communist Vietnam.

Instead, when Bob returned to Keller, he called the closest Catholic church, St. Elizabeth Anne Seton. He introduced himself to the priest as a fellow Christian who had just returned from Victnam, where he had met a remarkable Catholic priest ministering to the people at great personal risk to himself. The man needed Bibles. The priest at St. Elizabeth told him to come over; the two of them should get to know one another.

As Bob's church grew, so did its relationship with Vietnam. It was a two-way exchange. Youth from Vietnam would come for extended visits to Texas, always staying with families who were part of Bob's church. They weren't forced to come to church, but they generally did, and they participated in the youth group, too. Truth is, this made some of Bob's congregants nervous. These Vietnamese kids were, after all, Communists and atheists. Part of what Communists and atheists are taught to do is brainwash Christians, right? Could this be happening right in their church's youth group? Bob wasn't worried, and to ease the nerves of some of his more skittish congregants, he participated in a very personal way in the exchange program, taking Vietnamese kids into his home.

On September 11, 2001, as Bob listened to the surreal news of planes being hijacked and used as weapons on American soil, he was at the dining table with his Vietnamese exchange student. The first thing he did was make sure everyone he knew in New York City was OK. Then he said a prayer for his family and his country, and especially that young Vietnamese kid sitting at his table, whose parents on the other side of the world were probably out of their minds with worry, wondering what kind of crazy country they had sent their son to. Then he thanked God for guiding him to work with Communist Vietnam in the company of Catholic priests. Such peaceful, lovely people, those Vietnamese. Such a generous community, those Catholics. He was very grateful that his church had no relationships in the Middle East or with Muslims, a bloodthirsty lot if there ever was one. He wanted to live a good, long life, not get his head chopped off by a terrorist who prayed to a false god in a strange language.

It didn't take Bob long to discover the irony in his thinking. He had been taught to hate Communists, and above all Vietnamese Communists, but had found himself overcoming his fear through personal relationships. He had been taught to revile Catholics as followers of a false church, but had learned to admire the great personal risks they took for the opportunity to serve others. Perhaps the same thing would happen if he ever got the chance to work with Muslims. Bob was starting to see a new wisdom in his own faith, especially Jesus' command to love your enemy. "The whole point is that when you love someone, they stop being your enemy," he told me. "Maybe there's no such thing as enemies, just people we don't know and haven't met."

He got his chance a few months later, when a group approached him and asked if he and his church might do in Afghanistan what they had done in Vietnam. Bob agreed. He grew his beard out long, flew to Pakistan, and traveled with a group of Christians and a guide across into Afghanistan. Bob was pretty proud of himself; he felt both intrepid and enlightened, going into the heart of dangerous territory to love people that most Americans felt were enemies. No one else he knew had done anything even close to this. There was something that gave him pause, however: the schools and hospitals he saw in northern Pakistan were built and run by Catholics. "Holy cow," Bob thought to himself, "these people are everywhere."

When I visited Bob in Dallas in 2009, he brought me to a dinner and told me, "There's this Muslim guy you've got to meet. He's young, smart, politically active, a good Republican. You guys are a lot alike." And then he stopped and grabbed me by the shoulders. "You are a Republican, right? Don't forget, this is Texas."

"Let's go meet your guy," I told him. It turns out that the guy he was talking about was Suhail Khan, one of the first American Muslims Bob had come to know. After working on Capitol Hill for Congressman Tom Campbell, Suhail had worked in the Bush White House, where he had become friends with a lot of Evangelicals. After that, he had moved to Dallas. Figuring that after their experience with Vietnamese Communists Evangelicals there would be open to Indian Muslims, Bob asked Suhail to come speak at his church. It was such a positive experience that Bob began planning an international interfaith conference at his Southern Baptist church in Keller, Texas, in November 2010. I had the honor of speaking there.

Bob is convinced that building bridges between Evangelicals and Muslims is a priority similar to the Catholic–Evangelical understanding that took place in the late twentieth century. During the Cordoba House furor, Bob would tweet top-ten lists about Islam and Muslims: "What I Love about Muslims" and "What I've Learned from Islam."

But his highest hopes are in younger Evangelicals. Just as his generation viewed Catholics differently than their parents did, he hopes the next generation will view Muslims differently than the current one does. He addresses the issue directly in his speeches to younger pastors. One of those pastors came to see me in the fall of 2010, right around the time the anti-sharia referendum passed in Oklahoma. "I just got back from a conference," he told me, "and the keynote speaker, Bob Roberts, said one of the most Christian things

a pastor could do is build relationships with Muslims in our
city. He said that just as Christianity values compassion, so
does Islam. That is an alien idea to my congregation. But if
we're going to build relationships with Muslims, we will have
to know things we admire about Islam. Will you come do a
guest presentation at my church?"

Listening to this pastor in my office, I realized that Bob Roberts wasn't traveling the path of interfaith cooperation alone.
He was bringing others with him. As he changed personally,
he implemented changes in his church, and he spread the
gospel to his fellow pastors, knowing that each of them had
the power to impact large churches as well. Moreover, Bob
seemed to intuit that there were two key levers to changing
people's attitudes about other religions—the knowledge they
had about a particular religion, and the people they knew
from that community. I met Bob in 2009, after I'd been doing interfaith work for more than a decade, and silently mar-
veled at how much somebody outside the formal circles of
the movement had figured out in such a short period of time.
"Hmmm," I thought to myself, "maybe we should be implementing some of Bob's strategies at Interfaith Youth Core."
I only wish I'd met him earlier and learned from his approach
faster. It would have saved me a lot of headaches, especially
during the summer of 2010.

# PART II

# THE SCIENCE OF
# INTERFAITH COOPERATION

When the call came from Christiane Amanpour's producer in September 2010, a cheer went up at Interfaith Youth Core. Here was a journalist who knew what she was talking about when it came to religion and global affairs. She had reported from all over the world—Bosnia, Afghanistan, Gaza. She had seen religious conflict tear societies apart but had also seen faith-inspired people and organizations do heroic work. She had gotten up close and personal with real Muslim militants, and therefore knew it was laughable that people like Imam Feisal and Daisy Khan were being called radicals. And, especially from her experience in the Balkans, she was acutely aware that Muslims could well be the victims rather than the perpetrators of religiously motivated violence.

Christiane and I had met several times before. In fact, she had interviewed me for a CNN special called *Generation Islam*, encouraging me to speak of the hope I saw in the growing Muslim youth population around the world. Usually, when journalists asked me about Muslim youth, it was with an air of foreboding. I was struck that Christiane wanted my perspective on the promise rather than the threat of this rising generation.

I'd grown up watching *This Week*—it was part of the Sunday-morning ritual I had with my dad—so seeing George Will stroll into the green room, bowtie neatly in place, was a bit surreal for me. I caught up with the Reverend Rich Cizik and Irshad Manji, my copanelists for the segment on Islam in America, eavesdropping from time to time on the grilling Arianna Huffington was giving a White House economic adviser in the corner. Broadly speaking, Rich, Irshad, and I had the same view of the Cordoba House situation. Rich had recently made a statement at the National Press Club that Jesus would condemn a Florida pastor's plan to burn copies of the Qur'an. Irshad had written an op-ed in the *Wall Street Journal* stating that the opposition to Imam Feisal's interfaith center was misguided and then pivoting to emphasize that Muslims should use the media limelight as an opportunity to make Cordoba House the most progressive Muslim project the world had ever known. I had been opening my speeches with the line "Are we entering a new era of American prejudice?" and following it up with statistics and stories of how scared Muslims felt of their fellow US citizens. The typical format of a Sunday-morning talk show is for hosts to quote earlier statements of panelists and then ask them to expound. I was ready with more stories of Muslims as victims.

At the commercial break, we were hustled from the green room to the set. Christiane shot us a quick smile and then went right back to reading her notes. "Which one of us are you going to start with?" I gingerly asked. She lifted her head and raised her eyebrows at me as if to say, "We don't tell you those kinds of things ahead of time."

The first question went to Rich, the second to Irshad, each basically following the expected script. And then Christiane turned to me: "Eboo, you have done a lot in interfaith dialogue, trying to rebuild bridges here since the disaster of 9/11. What does this say to you, this fervor that's being whipped up, this rising tide of anti-Islamic sentiment in this country?" She ticked off the statistics I was going to use—one-third of Americans say Islam encourages violence; over half say they don't have a good understanding of the teachings and beliefs of Islam. Waving her hands and raising her voice, she asked point blank, "So, what has all your work done?"[1]

Thank God I'd gotten media training. The expert who put me through the drills emphasized three rules: Rule number one, don't listen to the question. If you make the mistake of hearing the question, don't let it bother you. Rule number two, have a positive message, know it cold, and be prepared to deliver it in twenty seconds or less. Rule number three, *SMILE*. Many people won't remember what you say, he told me, but they will remember your smile. If you get interrupted, repeat the cycle. When they ask you another question, repeat the cycle.

And that's exactly what I did. I beamed broadly for the cameras, talked about how in America the forces of inclusion always defeat the forces of intolerance, and told a story of a sixth-grade girl who donated her allowance to Interfaith Youth Core because she was bothered that too many people were being mean to Muslims. Christiane wasn't having it. "Well, that's wonderful," she said dismissively and went on to cite a recent *New York Times* article on how scared Muslims were feeling that summer, even more scared than they felt after 9/11.[2] And then she gave me a "What are you doing about that?" look. I dutifully put my smile back on and launched into another positive story. I would have kept smiling and pushing sunshine if Irshad had not interrupted.

It wasn't until I was on the flight back home that I really thought about Christiane's first question: *"What has all your work done?"* She wasn't asking me about how I felt as a Muslim living in America; she was asking about the impact of my work as president of Interfaith Youth Core. She was treating me as an agent, not a victim, effectively saying, 'Your job is not just to complain about religious prejudice; your job is to do something about it. The task of the organization you started, the claim of the movement you are part of, is to reduce prejudice and increase pluralism. How can you say you are doing your job if we keep seeing prejudice rise?" It was a perfectly reasonable question—an extremely important one, in fact—and I'm kind of glad that I successfully ignored it when she posed it to me on camera in front of 2 million viewers, because the truth is, it did bother me.

———

I'd gotten quite good at talking about religious prejudice, actually. I always had recent survey numbers on the tip my tongue in order to show just how pervasive the problem is in our society. I'd somberly tick off the percentages of Americans who said that Hinduism and Buddhism are "strange," who wanted Muslims to go through extra security at airports or don't believe they should serve on the Supreme Court, who, on account of a Mormon or secular-humanist presidential candidate's faith or their lack of one, would not vote for them. I'd make comparisons to the multicultural and feminist movements. Progress might not have come fast or gone far enough, but at least these issues were on people's radar screens. Take the election of 2008 as an illustration. For the most part, mainstream America was proud that we had African American and female candidates running for high office. It was certainly central to the media narrative about Barack Obama, Hillary Clinton, and Sarah Palin. When racism and sexism reared their ugly heads, the media cried foul. But the digs against the candidates' religions—the suggestion that because he is Mormon, Mitt Romney can't be president, that Sarah Palin is kooky because she attends an Evangelical church, that Barack Obama is a radical because his grandfather was Muslim—these were commonly stated and rarely called out. Part of the work of Interfaith Youth Core is to convince people that religious prejudice is a serious problem, and that it ought to be considered just as un-American as racism or sexism.

I'd also become expert at talking about how fast the interfaith movement is growing. A half-century ago, few cities had any organized interfaith activity. Today, dozens have some sort of initiative, everything from interfaith councils to festivals of faith. Religious denominations have invited leaders from other religions to give keynote addresses at their national gatherings, and local congregations have started interfaith exchange programs. Think tanks have commissioned task forces and issued reports. The United Nations launched a major interfaith initiative called the Alliance of Civilizations. Muslim and Christian theologians unveiled a document called "A Common Word Between Us and You."[3] Scores of scholarly books have been published, including one by Jonathan Sacks, the spiritual leader of the United Kingdom's largest Jewish synagogue organization.[4] Celebrated world-religions author Karen Armstrong used her TED Prize in 2008 to issue a "Charter of Compassion" calling all religions to redefine themselves by the shared, core value of loving others. Princes, prime ministers, and presidents have all, in various ways, lent their support to the interfaith cause. I remember standing in the Oval Office with President Obama at the first meeting of his inaugural Faith Council, when he spoke of the importance of interfaith cooperation as a way to strengthen America's civic fabric and to show the world that conflict between faiths is far from inevitable. "It's a rare opportunity," I would tell audiences at my public lectures, "when a grassroots movement becomes a global priority."

Every movement has its moment, and, at Interfaith Youth Core, we believed this was ours. We had grown rapidly from our first Ford Foundation grant of $35,000 and a handful of Chicago projects in 2002. Our activities now spanned the globe; our partners included everyone from Her Majesty Queen Rania of Jordan to the US State Department; our work was getting covered by major newspapers and cited by world leaders. If you opened a book or think tank report about interfaith cooperation written after 2005, there was a pretty good chance you would find a reference to Interfaith Youth Core. If there was an interfaith conference happening anywhere from Louisville to London, an IFYC staff member was very likely on the speakers' list. We had started the organization with two big ideas: that young people should be a priority, not an afterthought, in interfaith cooperation, and that social action should be central to interfaith efforts—enough already with the documents and ceremonies. Our rationale was simple: if religious extremism is a movement of young people taking action, and interfaith cooperation continues to be defined by senior theologians talking, we lose. In some quarters of the interfaith movement, those ideas were greeted with outward enthusiasm and backroom skepticism. Everybody knew, the whispers went, that young people aren't interested in religion—or anything else useful, for that matter. And what older people liked doing was having dinners, drafting declarations, and organizing panel discussions.

We had proved the skeptics wrong. A few years after that first Ford Foundation grant, our two basic ideas had become common practice within the interfaith movement and had received attention far beyond. In that Oval Office meeting with President Obama, he had mentioned both the importance of interfaith social action and the leadership of young people. On a visit to Chicago soon after Tony Blair stepped down as prime minister of the United Kingdom, Blair invited me to his suite at the Four Seasons Hotel to discuss plans for his new Faith Foundation. That conversation helped catalyze the foundation's Faiths Act Fellows program, in which thirty recent college graduates work in interfaith and international teams on social-action projects that have an impact on the United Nations initiative known as the Millennium Development Goals.

What would happen as more and more young people got involved in interfaith social-action projects? We believed this surge of interest would shape a society characterized by religious pluralism. In her work on interfaith cooperation, Harvard University scholar Diana Eck had made a crucial distinction between diversity and pluralism: diversity is simply the fact of people from different backgrounds living in close quarters.[5] Baghdad is diverse; Belfast is diverse; Bosnia is diverse. Each of those places, in recent memory, had also experienced serious interreligious violence. After the fall of Saddam Hussein, Baghdad had effectively become the site of a civil war fought between various groups of Iraqi Muslims wielding weapons and different interpretations of Islam. Where diversity is a fact, pluralism is an achievement—it means deliberate and positive engagement of diversity; it means building strong bonds between people from different backgrounds. IFYC's definition actually went one step further and laid out a three-part framework for pluralism: a society characterized by respect for people's religious (and other) identities, positive relationships between people of different religious backgrounds, and common action for the common good.

We set a grand goal for ourselves at IFYC: to make religious pluralism a social norm within the course of a generation. Just as environmentalism, volunteerism, and multiculturalism had permeated our society, altering the notion of what it means to be a good citizen, shifting the images we see in magazines and movies, changing patterns in schools and workplaces, so would the idea that people from different religious backgrounds should come together in ways that built respect, relationships, and common action. Every city would have a Day of Interfaith Youth Service, with thousands of religiously diverse young people cleaning rivers and building houses side by side, all inspired by a keynote address given by their mayor. Congregations that did not participate in interfaith exchanges would be considered out of the mainstream. Ordinary citizens would speak with pride of America's history of interfaith cooperation, in the same way as they talked about freedom, equality, and justice. Religious prejudice in political races would be considered as beyond the pale as blatant racism had become.

A big dream meant raising big money. I actually enjoyed this part of my job, in no small part because IFYC had experienced great success in fund-raising. My pitch basically revolved around interfaith cooperation being important. It was important because of the pervasiveness of religious prejudice and the destructiveness of religious violence. It was important because it had played an important part in history, from the civil rights movement in the United States to the struggle against apartheid in South Africa. It was important because lots of important people were talking about it. And IFYC was important because when important people talked about the importance of interfaith cooperation, they frequently talked about *us*. The State Department was sending our staff on speaking tours, cable news kept calling us for interviews, we ran cool projects all over the world. It was an inspiring narrative, and a remarkable number of the foundation program offices and individual philanthropists I met with found it compelling enough to help IFYC grow from that $35,000 Ford grant into a $4 million entity by 2009. That made us probably the largest interfaith organization in the United States, an impressive achievement for an outfit that opened its first office less than a decade ago and whose founder was neither a bishop nor a billionaire.

There was a certain New York City–based philanthropist I had been trying to get in front of for a year. "He loves programs that develop young people as leaders, especially through social action, and he has been talking more and more about the importance of religious diversity," IFYC board member Ron Kinnamon told me. "If you can energize him about our work, he's got the kind of money and clout to take us to the next level." Finally, I got my chance, a thirty-minute spot on his schedule. This was the big one.

I felt as ready as any organizational president has ever been to make a fund-raising pitch. I knew this man's favorite authors, I knew his other philanthropic investments, I came highly recommended by his personal friends. There are times when the pitch comes out perfectly and times when it feels a little shaky. On that morning in New York City, I was as on as I've ever been. I knew the mentoring programs he supported were domestic, so I talked about our activities in the United States. His work on the Millennium Development Goals was global, so I made sure to mention our partnerships with Tony Blair and Queen Rania. He was involved in American politics, and I managed to sneak in that Bill Clinton liked us. He supported youth programs, so I told stories of impressive projects IFYC student leaders had organized on college campuses. He was nodding and smiling; the moment to make the ask was getting close.

But first, he had a question. "Eboo," he asked, "how does Interfaith Youth Core measure effectiveness?"

OK, I thought, it looked like this man was listening, but maybe his mind was actually wandering a bit. No problem—he was busy, he had a lot of important things going on. I was happy to repeat. So I ran through the litany again, a little faster this time, lots of grassroots projects, lots of glow from the global stage; everything was growing, growing, growing. He nodded, and then he repeated his question using slightly simpler language: "How does your organization know that what you are doing is working?"

I tried a different tack this time. Religious prejudice was getting worse. Religious violence was getting worse. The institutions that were making religion a barrier of division or a bomb of destruction were getting lots of money. If the world wanted religion to be a bridge of cooperation, it had to invest more money in interfaith cooperation.

He leaned back in his chair. He was not nodding anymore, and he was not smiling. I realized that he had actually been paying very close attention the whole time, listening for a direct answer to his question about effectiveness. He wasn't hearing what he needed to hear. "You just used the word *investment*," he said. "Investments are what I do. The return on an investment in the business world is money. The return on an investment in the social world is impact. I invest in fields and organizations where I see effective work being done. The data in mentoring shows us that if an at-risk young person has a mentor, his or her chance of leading a successful life goes up significantly. The data in malaria shows us that bed nets, which, properly used, prevent people from getting bitten by malaria-carrying mosquitos, cost ten dollars each.[6] In each of those cases, I know precisely what impact my investment buys. I love the idea of interfaith cooperation, and I'm impressed by the sheer energy your organization brings to this issue. But I don't know the specific objectives of your activities, I don't know your definition of success, I don't understand how you've chosen your strategy, and I don't know the metrics you use to track progress. Bottom line: I can't measure the impact of my investment, and when that's the case, I don't invest."

He had caught me in a contradiction: if your organization is growing but the problem your organization claims to solve is growing faster, then maybe something you're doing is wrong.

How do we measure effectiveness in interfaith work? How do we track progress? What outcomes are we after, and how do we know we are reaching them? Frankly, I hadn't thought much about any of those things. When I thought about Interfaith Youth Core, words like *dream, passion,* and *vision* came to mind. Metrics were for the corporate guys who worked in cubicles, not the leaders of social movements. Actually, they were also for some of America's most perceptive observers of religion in public life.

The reason I could easily rattle off statistics on religious prejudice in America is because social scientists at universities like Harvard and Princeton and at organizations like Gallup and Pew had been gathering quantitative data about religious diversity for years. The most influential was Harvard University's Robert Putnam. In 1995, his book *Bowling Alone* introduced the term "social capital" into our nation's vocabulary.[7] The idea is simple: the activities that strengthen our civil society, from volunteering and voting to giving money to charity, are based on social networks and civic organizations. Such groups play a crucial role in any society, but America especially relies on the energies and involvement of its citizens in the civic sphere. As he later put it in a lecture, "Where levels of social capital are higher, children grow up healthier, safer, and better educated, people live longer, happier lives, and democracy and the economy work better."[8]

Probably the most important source of social capital in

America is religious communities. Putnam says that basically half of America's volunteerism, philanthropy, and associational membership is religiously based. This was especially dramatic during the abolition and civil rights movements, when large groups of religious people risked their lives to fight for things that they considered fundamentally religious values. But it goes on in less dramatic ways all the time, in the schools, hospitals, social-service agencies, and volunteer programs that religious communities run. Putnam writes, "[Faith communities] provide an important incubator for civic skills, civic norms, community interests, and civic recruitment. Religiously active men and women learn to give speeches, run meetings, manage disagreements, and bear administrative responsibility."[9] This is the good news. But there is bad news as well.

In his research, Putnam discovered something that he found extremely disturbing: diversity actually reduces social capital. In highly diverse areas in the United States, people report lower levels of confidence in local leaders, lower levels of confidence in their own influence, lower voting rates, fewer close friends and confidants, less likelihood of working on a community project, and lower expectations that other people in the area will cooperate together on community projects. About the only thing that people in highly diverse areas did more of was sit at home and watch television. Putnam concludes, "In more diverse communities, people trust their neighbors less . . . [and] appear to 'hunker down.'"[10] For a generation raised both to value civic engagement and celebrate diversity, it is more than a little sobering to learn that the data shows that the two are inversely correlated.

One problem is that America's social capital tends to be, in Putnam's term, bonded. Within religion, that means Catholics do things with other Catholics, Muslims with Muslims, Jews with Jews, and so on. Even when institutions founded by one community serve the broader public, they are typically run by that one community. In America's highly diverse society, Putnam much prefers what he calls bridged social capital—different religious groups that work together by, say, co-organizing volunteer programs. Not only does this bridging increase the good work being done for the broader society (the volunteering), it has the highly important effect of encouraging people from different backgrounds to work well together. In other words, bridging, or working together, both increases social capital and strengthens social cohesion.[11]

Diverse civil societies with high amounts of bonded social capital and deep distrust between different communities are in danger of everything from being silos to suffering civil wars. Effectively, you've got communities that encourage high participation within the group but little involvement with other groups or the broader society. What happens when those different groups decide they don't like one another? What happens when you take all that bonded social capital, all that powerful sense of in-group identity and those high levels of internal community participation, and release it in aggression toward other groups? That's when you get the religious violence of a Baghdad or a Belfast.

If a high amount of bonded social capital combined with tension between different groups in a diverse society is a recipe for a civil war, it is also true that bridged social capital can prevent such violence. In a study on India, Brown University social scientist Ashutosh Varshney asked the question "Why do some cities in India explode in inter-religious violence and others remain calm in similar circumstances?"[12] The answer, he discovered, is stunningly simple: cities that have what he calls networks of engagement—in Putnam's terms, civic associations that bridge social capital—remain peaceful. In cities that do not have organizations or activities in which people from different religious backgrounds regularly gather for good works, in times of interreligious tension, civil wars erupt.

America is among the most religiously diverse countries in human history and by far the most religiously devout nation in the West. How are we doing when it comes to bridging our religiously diverse social capital?

Social scientists measure America's religious diversity in three basic ways. The first and most common category is attitudes. This is a broad category, and there are many ways to ask questions about attitudes, but it generally comes down to a pretty basic sentiment: "Do you like Muslims/Jews/evangelicals/humanists?" The second category—relationships— is illustrated by questions like, "Do you know/work with/ have a friend of a different religion?" The final category is knowledge, exemplified by questions such as, "What religion is Shabbat associated with? In what faith do adherents fast from dawn to dusk for one month of the year?"

I knew this data well. I used it in my speeches and writings, and it helped me paint a picture of how bad the problem of religious prejudice is in our society. What I had failed to notice was that the data isn't just useful in presenting the problem; it actually shapes up to suggest a solution. The three measures—attitudes, relationships, knowledge—are actually deeply related. A 2007 Pew study found that 44 percent of people who *did not* know a Mormon had a positive attitude toward the Mormon community. Of people who *did* know a Mormon personally, 60 percent had favorable views. That's a 16-point difference. When the same question was asked regarding Muslims, the difference was even starker: only 32 percent of people who *did not* know a Muslim expressed favorable views toward the community, but of those who *did* know a Muslim, 56 percent had positive attitudes. That's nearly a 25-point difference—huge, really.[13]

In his most recent book, *American Grace*, written with David Campbell, Putnam calls this the My Friend Al Principle, which he explains like this: Say you are a beekeeper and your friend Al is a beekeeper. Apiculture brings you together, and through this shared activity, you learn that Al is an Evangelical Christian. Prior to meeting Al, you harbored a host of prejudices about Evangelicals, but if Al is a beekeeper and a good guy and an Evangelical, then maybe other

Evangelicals aren't so bad. Putnam and Campbell actually show strong statistical evidence for this principle—that people's regard for entire religious groups improves through a positive, meaningful relationship with even one member of that group, often formed through a common activity. Putnam and Campbell discovered that their data suggested something else: by becoming friends with Al the beekeeping Evangelical, not only did your attitude toward Evangelicals improve, so did your attitude toward Mormons and Muslims. They conclude, "We have reasonably firm evidence that as people build more religious bridges they become warmer toward people of many different religions, not just those religions represented within their social network."[14]

Clearly, relationships between people of different faiths have a profound impact on attitudes toward other faith communities. But that's not the only variable that makes a difference. There is also good evidence that knowledge of other traditions correlates strongly with positive attitudes. A 2009 Pew study found that those who reported a high familiarity with Islam—for example, knowing that Muslims call God Allah and that their holy book is called the Qur'an—are three times more likely to have favorable views of Muslims than those who report low familiarity.[15] A Gallup survey released the same year found a similarly strong correlation between knowledge of Islam and attitudes toward Muslims.[16]

But it's not just knowledge that matters; it's what you know—the type of knowledge—that counts the most. According to a recent Gallup Poll, only 2 percent of Americans say they have a great deal of knowledge about Buddhism, and 14 percent report feeling some prejudice towards Buddhists. Meanwhile, only 3 percent of Americans claim they have a great deal of knowledge about Islam, and yet 43 percent claim some prejudice towards Muslims.[17]

How is it that a little knowledge about Buddhism correlates with broadly positive feelings towards Buddhists, but a little knowledge about Islam is linked to frighteningly negative views of Muslims?

Here's my theory: In the minds of most people, entities as abstract and amorphous as religions are represented by the small piece of knowledge we have about that tradition. What people likely know about Buddhism is the figure of the Dalai Lama, and so it's hard for them to associate Buddhism with something terribly negative. When it comes to Islam, the images of terrorism come immediately to mind, and so people's view of an entire tradition is colored by an infinitesimally small but shockingly violent fringe.

That data point made me think about the man at the anti–Cordoba House rally carrying the sign that said, "All I Need to Know about Islam I Learned on 9/11." He didn't know much about a 1,400-year-old tradition with 1.5 billion believers, and the thing he did know was an act of horror.

This is just the tip of the iceberg in data about religious diversity. The more I studied this area, the more I started to see attitudes, knowledge, and relationships as three sides of a triangle. If you know some (accurate and positive) things about a religion, and you know some people from that religion, you are far more likely to have positive attitudes toward that tradition and that community. The more favorable your attitude, the more open you will be to new relationships and additional appreciative knowledge. A couple of cycles around this triangle, and people from different faiths are starting to smile at each other on the streets instead of looking away or crossing to the other side. A few more cycles—more knowledge, more friends, more favorable attitudes—and people are starting to say, "We ought to do something with those people who worship in that place called a mosque or a gurdwara down the street." To go back to the social science jargon, that's when bridging starts to happen, that's when social capital starts to grow, that's when social cohesion gets stronger.

But the triangle works the other way as well. You can run reverse cycles on it. People without much knowledge about other religions and with little contact with people from those communities are far more likely to harbor negative attitudes toward those traditions and communities. If movements emerge to fill those gaps in knowledge and relationships with negative information and ugly representations, people's attitudes go from negative to vociferously opposed. This is precisely what happened during the Cordoba House controversy. And that leads to community action as well—like arson attacks on mosque construction sites.

The joke about social scientists is that they run expensive research projects that generally end up proving common sense. In this case, it's true. You don't need to be a professor at Harvard or Princeton to know in your gut that positive relationships with people of other faiths and appreciative knowledge of their traditions will improve people's attitudes toward religious diversity. But it's one thing to feel something in your bones and another thing to have the data that proves beyond a shadow of a doubt that it is true. The data helps convince skeptics, but perhaps even more important, it focuses the efforts of activists. Now that we know that the key leverage points in building religious pluralism are appreciative knowledge and meaningful relationships, interfaith organizations can design their programs to increase these two factors.

This sounds innocent. All interfaith programs, at some level, seek to increase appreciative knowledge and facilitate positive, meaningful relationships, right? Sure, but once you have the science that shows what works and you make the decision to craft your programs to apply this science, you find yourself asking a whole different set of questions: How can we shape our program design so that we maximize for knowledge and relationships? What do we need to leave out of our programs, even if we loved doing some of those things, because they distract from our goal? Do we have instruments that can measure our progress? If we follow this science, we know that an interfaith panel that argues about the Middle East is not the most effective step to building positive relationships and spreading appreciative knowledge. Instead, a program that brings people from different religions together to discuss how their various faiths speak to the shared value of mercy is a more effective approach because it builds appreciative knowledge. Following it up by an opportunity where the audience can plan a concrete project applying mercy in small, religiously diverse groups where they can begin to form meaningful interfaith relationships is even better.

These were the conversations I started having with IFYC board members, especially one Tarek Elmasry, a director in the Chicago office of McKinsey and Company. (He's now running the Middle East region for McKinsey.) He liked nothing better than to talk about defining goals and measuring results. When he was convinced that I was serious about the science of interfaith cooperation, he committed to helping me design a strategy for implementing that science. He got us a McKinsey engagement team, pro bono. The team would spend its first weeks gathering data about the effectiveness of IFYC programs over the past five years, and then help us shape a plan for the next five years. Tarek himself would supervise the team. He promised to be personally involved. I had no idea how personal it would get.

"It's not working," Tarek told me. We were standing at the grill looking out over Lake Michigan in the backyard of his beautiful home on Chicago's North Shore. It was the middle of the summer, a perfect night to get the families together for a barbecue. "No shop talk," my wife had made me promise on the drive over. "Yep, of course," I said. What was there to talk about? Things were going great. I was in a celebratory mood.

Tarek wasn't. His wife had made him promise the same thing, but he had just gotten the first wave of data back from the McKinsey team working on the Interfaith Youth Core strategic plan, and he was not impressed.

"What are you talking about?" I said.

"It's not working," he repeated. "At current course and speed, it's going to take Interfaith Youth Core centuries to make interfaith cooperation a social norm, not decades, and that's only if you're lucky.

"Here are the facts," Tarek told me. "In any sector you work in—cities, campuses, US embassies abroad—you reach less than 5 percent of the total number of units. Within each city or campus or embassy, your penetration is unimpressive. So it's great that 150 people came to your lecture at the University of Illinois, but that's a campus of 35,000 people. And when 150 people come to your lecture in New York City—well, you do the math. Moreover, when we interviewed the people who attend IFYC speeches or trainings, they all say they find them inspiring—which is one of the bright spots in the data we've collected—but a year later, the vast majority say they haven't taken any significant interfaith action steps yet. So here's the bottom line: your staff is spread too thin across sectors, your programs don't reach enough people within sectors, and the people you reach don't take action. You want to know what my hypothesis about this is, Eboo?"

Actually, I really didn't, but Tarek kept rolling right along, flipping the steaks as he talked. "My hypothesis is that your organization is spread too thin across sectors because you see yourself as someone who generates cool new opportunities instead of someone who delivers impact. The embassy in Kazakhstan calls and asks for an IFYC staffer to come out, and you think to yourself, 'How awesome that people in Kazakhstan love Interfaith Youth Core—I must be doing something right,' and you send someone without any thought about the purpose of the trip. And the reason that people don't take action after IFYC programs is because you don't give them a clear road map of what it means to be an interfaith leader and what action to take. You make ten different suggestions, whatever new ideas you've been reading about in the *New Yorker*. When you tell people to do ten things, the chances are they'll do nothing.

"And you want to know why I think that's happening?" I didn't even try to stop him this time. "It's because of you. You talk too much and you say too many different things, both within your organization and outside of it. You like to sound interesting, full of new ideas. Well, that's great for cocktail parties and newspaper columns, but it's bad if you want to build an organization that leads a social movement. As a leader, you lack focus and discipline. And your organization has taken on that personality. *It* lacks focus and discipline."

This was too much for me. I started to yell. I knew I was going to hear it from my wife afterward, but I just could not sit there and take this anymore. Was he not reading all the glowing press reports on IFYC? Did he not know about all the awards we were winning?

"Sizzle is good," Tarek said in a maddeningly slow, patient voice. And then he repeated the same lines: The data showed that we were not on track to achieve our goal—nowhere near, actually. For us to have any hope of making interfaith cooperation a social norm within the space of a generation, we had to stop generating scattered opportunities to do interfaith work and focus on impact. Instead of spreading ourselves thin across sectors, we ought to focus in one area where we could make a measureable change. The sector ought to see interfaith cooperation as a priority and to view itself as playing a vanguard role in American society. As we reached a tipping point within that sector, it would not only serve as a model for the rest of the society but also produce leaders who would directly influence other sectors. With respect to leadership development, IFYC needed to be clear about what we thought people who attended our workshops should do after they left, design the workshop to inspire and equip them to do it, and create a campaign that encouraged lots of people to take that action together.

"Steaks are done," he said, and smiled.

I wanted to throw him into the lake, but he'd already walked inside.

The hardest thing for a leader to take is criticism in the area he thinks he's an expert. I complained that Tarek was robbing us of our creativity, that he was too enamored of his own consultant-think. But I couldn't dispute the facts that he was laying out in front of me. It was true: we had not achieved critical mass in any sector, and people who went through our trainings said they left inspired but didn't launch projects at the rate we had hoped. It was also true that I had a healthy opinion of my own talent for generating ideas and opportunities. I had been invited to speak at Stanford, Yale, Princeton, the Clinton Global Initiative, TED; I was on an advisory committee for the Council on Foreign Relations and the board of the Chicago Council on Global Affairs; I was writing for the *Washington Post* and getting quoted in the *New York Times*. I was the interfaith ideas guy.

This was something I used to pride myself on. My favorite questions were the ones from left field—the further out the better. I loved it when someone in the audience stood up and talked about a random social problem and asked how interfaith cooperation could help solve it. From deforestation in Brazil to drug addiction in Buffalo, I've heard them all, and then some. I remember speaking to the cabinet and board of a small college in Iowa about the power of interfaith work, and being somewhat surprised when the board chair said, "We've got a big teen-pregnancy problem in this community. Can your organization help us do something about that?" I'd never thought about teen pregnancy and interfaith cooperation before, but that didn't prevent me from musing aloud for five minutes on what might be done.

In addition to telling the leaders of nonprofit organizations what new social problems they should take on, people also love telling us all the new places we ought to be working. You should be writing curriculum for preschools, people have told me, more scolding than suggesting. You should be running workshops in prisons, holding interfaith rallies in Portland, opening an office in Portugal. There seems to be no place on the planet that does not desperately need some version of an Interfaith Youth Core program. Of course, these statements spoke directly to my ego. See how valuable and necessary people think your work is! My typical reaction was to go with the flow: "Let me think about how we might do that." And when I came up with a brilliant plan, I called my staff together and started outlining it on the white-board. These used to be known as the Eboo-chasing-another-unicorn-down-a-dark-path sessions. "Ah, yes, but isn't she beautiful?" I would respond.

For Tarek, this was precisely the problem. If interfaith co-operation could be morphed into anything, then it was really about nothing. If interfaith cooperation went easily every-where, then its impact was really nowhere. The goal of Inter-faith Youth Core wasn't to be an organization that proposed an interfaith solution to every conceivable social problem in every possible geography; it was to build understanding and cooperation between people from different faith back-grounds where it worked. For Tarek, responding to left-field questions and riding out random opportunities wasn't an in-teresting quirk of Interfaith Youth Core. It revealed an orga-nization that either didn't know what it was doing or didn't have the integrity to do what it was saying. These practices were not just for corporate consultants; they were also fol-lowed by some of the nonprofit leaders I respected most.

When I was in college, one of my professors handed me a book titled *Who Will Teach for America?*[18] "It's about a young social entrepreneur named Wendy Kopp who had an idea for a domestic teaching corps when she was in college," he told me. I devoured the book, and I became a devotee of Wendy's. When her memoir *One Day, All Children . . . : The Unlikely Triumph of Teach Across America and What I Learned Along the Way* came out a few years later, I read it three times and underlined about half the book.[19] She had done what I wanted to do: have a big idea and make it reality. When I met her some years later, I asked her to recount the story of the moment the idea had hit her, how she had convinced her par-ents that she was going to chase her dream instead of a cor-porate job, what those first staff meetings and fund-raising conversations had been like. I told her that I was trying to follow in her footsteps with Interfaith Youth Core.

"I'll tell you a little secret," she said. "Everybody wants to hear the story of the idea, but having the idea is actually the easy part. The hard work is setting goals and building an organization that accomplishes those goals. Your organization exists to get results. Define those results clearly and pursue them relentlessly."

Part of the promise of the growing science in religious diversity is that it provides a plan for making interfaith cooperation a social norm. If we train a critical mass of leaders to create enough spaces that expand the number of positive, meaningful encounters between people from different religions and programs that increase people's appreciative knowledge of other religious traditions, the studies tell us that people's attitudes toward other faith communities will improve. As people's attitudes improve, they will seek more interfaith friendships and interfaith literacy. When we work the attitudes-relationships-knowledge interfaith triangle, we build connections between people from different backgrounds. These connections become the networks of engagement that prevent social conflict and create the bridging social capital that address social problems.

This all looks very logical as a flowchart on a whiteboard. My wife was not so impressed. "Every time you say 'interfaith cooperation as a social norm' or 'the science of the interfaith triangle,' you have to buy me something—something *nice*," she told me. She was being cute, but she was also signaling something more serious. I was once an organizational president who told majestic stories of how interfaith leaders in the past had shaped some of history's most inspiring moments— Gandhi and Abdul Ghaffar Khan in India, Martin Luther King Jr. and Abraham Joshua Heschel in Selma, Farid Esack and Desmond Tutu in South Africa—and told young people today that the next chapter in the narrative of religious pluralism was theirs to write. I had become someone who kept repeating the terms *science, strategy,* and *social norm.* It wasn't just my wife who had a problem with it. I could see eyes glaze over in my public talks when I started explaining the science of interfaith cooperation. Even some IFYC staff complained about the work not being inspiring anymore.

I started to get frustrated. "People," I wanted to yell (and probably did, at some points), "do you not realize that if we fail to create rigorous systems for applying this science and evaluating our programs, our movement will deserve the most common insults of the skeptics: that we are well-meaning and ineffective." But I knew in my heart that they were right. This work is either inspiring, or it doesn't exist.

If interfaith cooperation becomes about applying a science, does it lose the beauty of its craft? If interfaith cooperation becomes about executing a strategy, does it ignore the power of people's stories? It was a day spent with one of the world's most celebrated interfaith leaders that reinforced for me how much of an art it is to apply a science well.

# THE ART OF INTERFAITH LEADERSHIP

"I'm inspired," I heard the man say. "But I wonder if he's just preaching to the choir?" We were walking out of an arena in Chicago where His Holiness the Dalai Lama had just done a teaching on interfaith cooperation in front of about eight thousand people. "Pretty big choir," I thought to myself. "A choir that size, it could do a lot in this world."

About every other speech I give, somebody stands up and says, "Thanks for your talk, but didn't you just preach to the choir?" They mean it as a mild rebuke, but increasingly I'm not so sure I see the metaphor the same way.

One of the striking things about the furor around Cordoba House was the consistency and pattern of language used by a wide group of people:

Radical Imam
Terrorist Command Center
Oppress women
Sharia sharia sharia
Stealth jihad
Taqiyya
Replace Constitution
Sharia sharia sharia

Verse, chorus, verse, chorus. It was a large choir singing

a song loudly. They knew every word and every note, and every day they grew in size and increased in volume. How did they learn that song? Well, there was Newt Gingrich on television using and twisting terms like *sharia* and "stealth jihad." Robert Spencer was doing it in books, Brigitte Gabriel in her public speeches, Franklin Graham in his television appearances, Pamela Geller on her blog, David Yerushalmi in his anti-sharia legislation. These were the preachers. Some even wore collars.

The people who logged on to their websites, read their books, listened to their sermons, sent checks to their organizations—they were the choir. Why were they so effective in creating a climate of fear around Muslims? Simple. *They sang the song the preachers taught them.* Some people who heard the song found the music compelling and joined the choir, so the choir got larger and the song of religious prejudice got louder. The choir members with the most dedication and the best voices were picked out and given special training—preacher training. They were sent on the road to start new choirs. More preachers, new choirs, louder song, repeat cycle. Pretty good way to build a movement, actually.

The follow-up to asking, "Aren't you just preaching to the choir?" is stating that the people who really need to hear the message didn't come to this presentation. The assumption is that social change happens when you go find the toughest problems, and that the people who come to the talk or show up at the activist meeting should somehow be disqualified precisely because they are interested in the issue. Increasingly, social-change theory is saying the opposite: the trick is not in finding the toughest problem, it's identifying the people who embody the solution and helping them spread it. Preaching, if you will, to the choir.

In their book *Switch,* social-change scholars Chip and Dan Heath illustrate this principle with the story of Jerry Sternin's work for Save the Children in Vietnam in the early 1990s. Sternin's objective was to improve nutrition in the country. He didn't speak the language, he wasn't given a plan, and he wasn't particularly welcomed by the government, which gave him six months to make a difference and stern warnings not to rock any boats. The analysis papers Sternin read on Vietnam and malnutrition were uniformly pessimistic: malnutrition couldn't be solved unless sanitation was improved, poverty was alleviated, education became universal. Sternin labeled this information TBU—True But Useless. His job was not to add to the literature of why malnutrition was such a big problem, it was to find a solution.

Sternin started going to poor rural villages and asking a simple question: Were there examples of typical families whose children were healthier than the rest? Once he found those families, he went about figuring out what they were doing differently than others. It turns out that the mothers of the healthier kids were doing a few simple extra things—mixing greens and tiny shrimp in with the basic rice, and providing four smaller meals a day rather than two larger ones.

Now that he knew what worked, Sternin's challenge was to figure out how to spread it. Creating a big conference and doing a PowerPoint presentation on strategies for nutritional success would have looked good in memos back home but would have done little to improve nutrition in Vietnam. Instead, Sternin devised a model in which the mothers of healthy children shared their methods with the others. It was simple, and it fit right into the fabric of village life. He suggested that the village mothers cook together, with the mothers of healthy children showing the others how to mix in the greens and shrimp, and how to prepare smaller portions that their children would eat more often. The strategy was highly successful. Six months after Sternin arrived in the village, 65 percent of the kids were better nourished. The program spread to 265 villages, impacting 2.2 million people.

Jerry Sternin found people who already knew the song of good nutrition in Vietnam. He helped them sing it louder and to teach it to larger choirs.[1]

———

Where was the song of interfaith cooperation during the Ground Zero Mosque crisis? I know it existed, but it was hard to hear. That's because most interfaith work isn't actually a large choir singing the same song; most interfaith work is more like a chamber ensemble. Chamber music is a classical form meant for the intimate quarters of a palace chamber—basically, a handful of highly trained musicians playing for a small group of their friends. It is beautiful, it is deep, it is intimate, and it is very, very soft. It is the type of interfaith work described in *The Faith Club,* a popular book written by a Muslim, a Christian and a Jew about the group the authors formed to discuss their spiritual journeys with one another after 9/11.[2] It inspired many more faith clubs around the country, small groups of people sharing the rich details of their personal spiritual journeys in intimate settings. It is one of the most common formats for interfaith work.

The vast majority of people I know who get involved in interfaith work do so because of their personal spiritual journeys: their best friend or their boyfriend is of another religion, a teacher they admire or an aunt they love calls God something else, they read *The Autobiography of Malcolm X* and want to know more about Islam—or, like me, they read Dorothy Day's autobiography, *The Long Loneliness,* and are inspired by how her Catholic faith motivated a life of justice. There are few things more personal than the question of how we view the divine and how we relate to those who understand the divine differently. What happens when we find beauty in faiths we were raised to think were wrong, even evil? What happens when we discover that someone else lives the values of our faith better than we do, *and they are of a different faith?* What happens when we rely on our faith to help us through a catastrophe and find people from other faiths doing the same thing, finding a similar solace in different prayers? This is what *The Faith Club* is about. It's an eloquent book that touched a lot of people and inspired a lot of important conversations.

As faith clubs took off, I noticed something interesting— my own book, *Acts of Faith,* started selling better.[3] It turns out that a lot of faith clubs were choosing it as their common reading. "Of course," I thought to myself, "it's a book about how my personal spiritual journey as a Muslim was shaped by a Catholic activist, a Jewish poet, and a Buddhist monk." Faith clubs were using it as a vehicle to spark conversation about personal spiritual journeys among their own members. I had provided the score for their chamber ensemble. It made me proud, but it also left me wondering: beautiful as chamber music is, it is not a language easily acquired by large groups of people, it is not particularly suited for rallying the masses, and it certainly cannot be heard above the thrash metal of religious prejudice. It is neither the right theme song nor the best format for a social movement. During the furor around Cordoba House, as Pamela Geller was putting large "Leave Islam" advertisements on the sides of New York City buses—the sheet music of religious prejudice for millions to learn on their way to work—I imagined thousands of Americans speaking in a sacred whisper about appreciating each other's spiritual journeys within the intimate confines of their faith clubs.

The more I thought about the Dalai Lama's visit to Chicago, the more I viewed it as a perfect example of preaching to the choir, and moreover doing it in a manner that seemed to follow the science of the interfaith triangle. The Dalai Lama can obviously assemble a pretty large choir, but still, he was strategic about how he went about organizing it. The day after his talk at the basketball arena in Chicago, he did a panel discussion with three American religious leaders—Professor Ingrid Mattson, the former president of the Islamic Society of North America; Reverend Peg Chemberlin, the president of the National Council of Churches; and Rabbi Michael Lerner, a well-known progressive Jewish leader. I was the moderator for the discussion, and as I talked with some of the audience members who attended, I realized that there were Christians, Jews, Muslims, and Buddhists who had come to see *their* religious leader interacting with the Dalai Lama. By putting those leaders on the same panel, the Dalai Lama had gotten Chicago's religiously diverse communities in the same theater together. In other words, he had created a religiously diverse choir. In the framework of the interfaith triangle, he had shaped a powerful opportunity for positive, meaningful encounters between people of diverse religious faiths.

After gathering the choir, the job of the preacher is to teach us the song. The content of the Dalai Lama's teaching in Chicago was based on his book, *Toward a True Kinship of Faiths: How the World's Religions Can Come Together*, a book that is basically the lyrics of interfaith literacy. The Dalai Lama begins with a beautiful story about Thomas Merton's visit to his residence in Dharamsalla in 1968. The two monks compare their robes, their meditation practices (Merton woke up at 2:30 a.m., an hour earlier than the Dalai Lama, to begin his prayers), the relationship between ritual, values, and spirituality in their respective traditions. That personal narrative provides a doorway for the Dalai Lama to discuss Tibet's history of interfaith encounter, with a special focus on the story of an Italian Jesuit who spent enough years in dialogue with Buddhist monks that he wrote a lengthy text about the value of comparative religious study *in Tibetan*. The Dalai Lama picks up the thread of the meeting with Merton again in his chapter on Christianity, where he emphasizes "the centrality of the compassionate ideal of relieving others from suffering as a key motivation in both Buddhism and Christianity."[4] In his early brush with Christianity, the Dalai Lama had found the stark and bloody image of Jesus on the cross somewhat startling. Merton points him to the picture of the Virgin Mary cradling the Baby Jesus and the verses in the Bible that speak of love, and emphasizes to the Dalai Lama that all of Christianity—the sacrifice, the blood, the cross—has to be understood in light of that single, central value: love.

In his visit to Chicago, the Dalai Lama did not stop at simply teaching the lyrics. He made sure the choir, at least the panelists on stage, sang the song. He wanted to hear about our personal friendships with people from different religions. Could we relate stories of service projects we had done with people of other faiths? He spoke about the lessons he had learned about compassion from other religions. Could the religious leaders on stage point to something they admired in other traditions? Was there a teaching central to our religions that we had found enriched by other faiths, in the way that he had learned about compassion from the image of the Virgin Mary holding the Baby Jesus? In a world where all the noise is about faith as a barrier of division and a bomb of destruction, the Dalai Lama had us singing the song of faith as a bridge of cooperation.

In his closing, the Dalai Lama turned to each panelist and gave us a charge: Ingrid Mattson should focus on involving women in interfaith cooperation, Peg Chemberlin should lift up the example of Jesus as a model of compassion, Michael Lerner had to write about the Middle East in a way that embraced the humanity of both Palestinians and Israelis, and I was to continue to energize young people, especially Muslim youth, to join the interfaith movement. He was basically telling us that being in the choir was great, singing the song of interfaith cooperation was great, but we all had to go a step further. He wanted us to become preachers and start new choirs.

When the event was over, people didn't rush for the doors. They lingered and chatted, shook hands and exchanged greetings with people they'd never met before. A religiously diverse audience felt like it had a special moment not just with a great spiritual leader but with one another. I overheard one person call the event "a reorientation of my spirit." The social science term for that feeling is "attitude change." This was not the time to tell people how perfectly the Dalai Lama had followed the interfaith triangle, but I couldn't help noticing it myself. The part I was most struck by is how naturally he had advanced the most intimidating part of the triangle—the knowledge side.

The Dalai Lama's teachings in Chicago were an example of what I've started to call interfaith literacy. It's a concept that first occurred to me after I read Stephen Prothero's important book, *Religious Literacy: What Every American Needs to Know—But Doesn't.* Prothero argues that all citizens ought to know basic terms and reference points in major religions to participate in our religiously diverse and devout society. He is careful to say this is not about liking other religions; it is only about knowing their basics. Part of the reason for this emphasis is that Prothero wants religious literacy taught in public high schools, and feels that a subject as loaded as teaching about religion, while it may be perfectly legal, is likely to provoke a sharp reaction. Exhibiting a studied neutrality—what Prothero calls the "just the facts" approach—is the best chance of disarming the skeptics.

But the Dalai Lama was going a step further. He wanted people to do more than recognize the terms of the discourse in a religiously diverse society. He wanted people to like one another, learn from each other, build bridges, form friendship, work together, *thrive* together. He was advancing a knowledge base that served this end. The stories he was telling were about the parts of different religions he admired and found beautiful—the call to prayer in Islam, Hinduism's Kumbh Mela festival, the example of St. Francis in Christianity, Judaism's Kabbala, the spiritual discipline of observant Jains, the passages on peace in the Sikh scripture, the architectural magnificence of the Baha'i Temple in New Delhi. The Dalai Lama wasn't interested in becoming an expert in other religions; he wanted to be an expert in what he loved about other religions.

The first part of interfaith literacy is an appreciative knowledge of other traditions. This means learning about what we admire in other faiths, the beauty in their texts and rituals, the contributions that their members have made to our society, the type of knowledge that fosters friendships and facilitates work together. The second part of interfaith lit-

eracy is the ability to identify values that all religions share—
compassion, mercy, hospitality, service. The third part is an
understanding of the history of interfaith cooperation in our
nation and our world. The final part is developing your own
theology of interfaith cooperation, based on the texts, stories, and rituals of your own tradition. Taken together, these
four parts are a knowledge base for cultivating pluralism in a
religiously diverse society.

The part that struck me most in *Toward a True Kinship of
Faiths* was the material on Islam. The Dalai Lama begins by
effectively admitting not knowing much about the tradition
until the attacks of 9/11, and in the aftermath finding himself
disturbed by the constant news reports of terrorism committed by Muslims, and the peculiar alliance between Muslim
extremists and Muslim haters to try to prove to the world
that Islam is inherently violent. Common sense said this
couldn't be true. Religions don't spread around the world,
last for nearly 1,500 years, and attract 1.5 billion followers
when they are only about violence. But simply being convinced that the media portrayal was skewed was not enough.
And so the Dalai Lama undertook a program of study that
effectively gave him interfaith literacy about Islam.

He read the poems of Rumi and the history of tolerance in the Muslim tradition. He visited mosques and went
to Muslim events. He searched in the Qur'an and the Ha-
dith literature for examples of compassion. He found shared
values between Islam and Buddhism and reviewed the history of interfaith cooperation between the two communities. He concluded, "Since God [in Islam] is characterized
as the Compassionate and the Merciful, in my understanding, the faithful are actually offering an absolute submis-
sion to the ideal of universal compassion. . . . In my own
Buddhist tradition, there is a similar practice in which one
offers one's entire being as a servant to the embodiment
of compassion."[5]

Chicago wasn't the only American city where the Dalai
Lama came to talk about interfaith cooperation. In the last

few years, I've participated in events with him in New York City, San Francisco, and Bloomington, Indiana. I noticed that the Dalai Lama seems to prefer a two-part format. Frequently, he'd hold an intimate meeting with a smaller group of leaders, discussions in which he could ask pointed questions about the other faith and offer more complex ideas about Buddhism. And then he'd hold larger teachings in which he would hold up, for a mass audience, the commonalities he'd recently discovered. I started to view the two parts as serving two very different but connected goals: In the smaller meeting, the Dalai Lama was adding to his own song on interfaith cooperation and helping his fellow preachers improve their song by contributing to their knowledge on Buddhism. In the larger meeting, he was teaching the song to a large choir. Both were necessary for effective interfaith leadership. The intimate settings were where the Dalai Lama got his own inspiration and knowledge, and the larger settings were where he inspired and enlightened a large group of others.

Reflecting on this strategy helped me understand the power and purpose of faith clubs and interfaith book groups. These are the spaces where the preachers of the movement improve their own interfaith literacy, develop their most intimate interfaith relationships, and keep their own inspiration flowing. Without these spaces, the song gets stale and the preachers get tired. But if the preachers don't create larger formats, invite in those bigger choirs, teach them the basic melody and lyrics, encourage them to sing loud and proud, then the song of interfaith cooperation doesn't exist in the world.

In Bloomington, as the Dalai Lama was walking out from his intimate meeting with Muslims to the larger teaching he was preparing to offer, he told me the story of his earliest Muslim friendship. It was with a clock repairer in Tibet, when the Dalai Lama was just a boy. His Holiness used to be so rough with his pocket watch that he broke it frequently. The best clock repairer in Lhasa happened to be a Muslim, and he would come dutifully to the palace when the attendants called and said the young Dalai Lama had broken his watch yet again. One day, the old man gave the Dalai Lama some advice on gentleness: "Treat the watch as if it is a raw egg," the man cautioned. "Gently, gently." The man offered the lesson with such gentleness himself that the Dalai Lama began to view him as an embodiment of that quality, and when he thought about Islam in the days after 9/11, he reflected on his memory of this Muslim watch repairer instead of focusing on the images of the terrorists.

There was something about that story of an uncommon friendship, and the way the Dalai Lama told it, that made me think of Chris Stedman. Like the Dalai Lama, Chris is an interfaith leader, but he doesn't have religious robes, a religious title, or even a religious commitment. Chris is an atheist, a gay atheist, with a body full of tattoos and a face covered in piercings. He's also one of the best interfaith leaders I know. And that's because he and the Dalai Lama share the key talent in interfaith leadership: the ability to build relationships across difference, and tell stories about these relationships that inspire others to do the same.

There is a moment in the middle of Chris's forthcoming book *Faitheist* that about took my breath away.[6] Chris is living in Bemidji, a small town in the northern part of Minnesota near the headwaters of the Mississippi River. The nearest big city, Fargo, is several hours away. In the winter, the snow piles up so high he can't see out of the bedroom window in his garden apartment.

Chris arrived there hoping to escape his past, to find a place where, as he writes, "I didn't run into ghosts from my former Christian life that reminded me of the years I spent hating myself for being queer and unable to change it." By the time he was a student at Augsburg College, Chris's disgust with religion had come to define him as deeply as his Evangelical faith once had. To a group of fellow students whom he knew to be believing Christians, he described getting a Bible verse tattooed on his leg as the single stupidest thing he'd ever done, and derived a peculiar pleasure from the offense he caused.

Chris had come to Bemidji because he wanted to live in a place where he could slow down and reflect, form deep relationships with small-town neighbors, take the first steps down a career path of service. He found a job working as a direct-service professional for adults with developmental disabilities at a social services agency run by Lutherans. (Yes, he is self-aware enough to note the irony.) His closest relationship was with a man named Marvin, a man who couldn't talk and who could barely sign. They found other ways to communicate: Marvin would pretend to sock Chris in the jaw, and Chris would fall down and bounce back with his dukes up and say, "This isn't over yet, buddy," sending Marvin into gales of laughter. Chris watched movies with Marvin, sat with him for hours just keeping company, read to him from his favorite books.

One day, Marvin brought Chris into his room and placed in his hands one of his most precious possessions: his prayer book. He wanted Chris to read from it. Chris hesitated for a second. Perhaps he was reminded of all those nights he lay awake searching through Scripture for verses, hoping to find one that would make him feel loved for what God made him. Perhaps he was reminded of the time when, in a drunken rage, he kicked in the glass panel of a church sign. But neither longing nor anger overcame him now. This moment was about what it means to be a friend, about expressing care for something Marvin values. Chris read Marvin a prayer. Marvin, normally tense, let his arms relax. Perhaps he sensed that some deep personal bridge had been crossed in his presence. He pressed his face tightly to Chris's blue flannel shirt and kept it there for a long time.

This is the beginning of Chris's path to interfaith leadership, the moment when he makes the decision to discover what about faith would mean so much to his friend Marvin instead of focusing on those dimensions of religion that frustrate him personally. This is when Chris realizes that the loudest preachers in the choir of his identity group, atheism, have been saying that such friendships are suspect because all people of faith are purveyors of prejudice and ticking time bombs of extremism. Chris decides to write a different atheist song and teach it to the choir of his own community. It is an atheist song that doesn't hate religion; it is one that loves people. It is a song that says the atheist movement ought to be standing up for those who are suffering, and working in solidarity with those who are different. It is a song that Chris sang loudly and clearly during the Cordoba House crisis.

"[Cordoba House] is under attack because of how demonized Muslims are in America, plain and simple," Chris wrote. "Many Americans see nothing but godless, immoral, savage heathens when they think of Muslims. As a community comparably cast, we should empathize and come to their defense. Defending their freedom is defending our own."[7] It is precisely because atheists value freedom of religion ("because of it, we are able to choose none," he wrote), and know what it means to be marginalized as a result of their views, that they ought to be on the front lines in support of those who are having their religious choice demonized.

Chris teamed up with two IFYC alumni, Josh Stanton and Frankie Fredericks, a rabbinical student and a born-again Christian, respectively, to organize one of the largest gatherings in America in support of Cordoba House. On the tenth anniversary of 9/11, over a thousand people from different faith backgrounds (including a healthy contingent who, like Chris, proudly proclaimed they had no faith at all) gathered in the rain in Lower Manhattan for the Liberty Walk, listening to speakers, chanting slogans, and marching to support the idea that Muslims (like everybody else) should be able to build their institutions anywhere on America's sacred ground. Somebody on the street told Chris that the whole country was against them. That just made Chris think of how hard past generations had worked to protect religious pluralism, and how proud he was to be working with friends like Frankie and Josh to extend that value into our era.

In a way, they served as Chris's intimate interfaith book club. They were the people he had the deepest relationships with, the ones who most inspired him. But what makes the Liberty Walk noteworthy is how they collectively inspired so many others. How they organized a choir of over a thousand people to sing the song of religious pluralism in a place that had, a decade before, suffered from the death chants of religious extremism, and for several weeks prior, the thrash metal of religious prejudice.

The future of pluralism in America depends more on the Chris Stedmans, the Josh Stantons, and the Frankie Fredericks than on the Dalai Lamas. First, there just aren't that many Dalai Lamas. Secondly, when it's only the cosmic giants we hold up as exemplars, it creates the sense that interfaith leadership is for otherworldly creatures. When Chris or Josh or Frankie is onstage telling stories about his friendships with people of different faiths, I watch the faces of young people in the audience light up, and I know behind those eyes they are thinking, "I relate to that story. I can do this, too." That's a key step in growing preachers—having people in the choir relate to you.

One thing about music, when you diagram it out, it can feel dry and expert, like the worst stereotypes of science. But once the notes start coming through your mouth, it becomes an art, and that art moves people. The same is true for the song of interfaith cooperation. There is a science to the interfaith triangle and how it maps to academic concepts like bridging social capital and building networks of engagement. But interfaith preachers who speak only of the science will find that the choir has gone elsewhere. That's because the application of the science, like actually singing the notes of the score, sounds and feels like something else entirely.

Forming a relationship with someone of a different tradition is an art. Reflecting on that relationship in a way that expands the way you understand your own path is an art. Telling the story of that friendship so that it changes others, that is an art as well. Creating spaces where people can form their own interfaith relationships—art. Taking passages from Scripture, stories from contemporary culture, moments from our own lives, weaving them together into a song that helps people glimpse the possibilities of pluralism—all of it, an art. Assembling a choir, teaching them the song, making sure they sing, nudging them to stay on key, allowing the best members to riff and solo, pulling them out and training them to be preachers, sending them off to start their own choirs—the whole thing, an art.

Chris, Josh, and Frankie first heard about the idea of interfaith cooperation in college. It's the key space in our society where a choir of idealistic young people from a range of backgrounds come together to form their vocations, participate in a diverse community, and acquire a knowledge base that will help them be leaders in the world beyond. It is the cathedral where I have been blessed to do the vast majority of my interfaith preaching. Though there are many sectors in our society where interfaith cooperation is relevant and necessary (houses of worship, neighborhoods, hospitals, and cities, to name a few), I believe college campuses play a uniquely powerful role. As Chilean sociologist Eugenio Tironi suggested, the kind of society we seek is intimately connected to the type of education we offer.[8] If we believe in a nation where people from different faith backgrounds live in equal dignity and mutual loyalty, we will have to make the teaching and practice of interfaith cooperation a priority on our nation's campuses.

In the question-and-answer session after a public talk I gave at Northwestern University, a student got up and asked, with a hint of indignation in her voice, "It's great that you're giving this speech about interfaith leadership at Northwestern, but when are you going to bring this message to the small town I'm from in Kentucky, a place where they'd rather meet a Martian than a Muslim?"

I was about to accept that challenge when the obvious occurred to me: What if every student in that room said, "Come to my hometown?" Movements aren't built by a single person running himself ragged through a thousand places; they're built when a diverse network of people internalize a central message and are able to communicate it effectively to their various communities.

And what did I know about a small town in Kentucky, anyway? My favorite speaking engagements are on college campuses; my favorite teaching opportunities are at seminaries and divinity schools. That's where my interfaith journey had begun. And perhaps through the law of like attracting like, the same was true for much of our staff at IFYC. We are familiar with the higher-ed patois, we know what it feels like both to be and to mentor student leaders. It was clear—and the McKinsey analysis confirmed it—that the sector where the Interfaith Youth Core could make the highest impact was in universities and seminaries. How we do it is the subject of the next two chapters.

But here is what I told that student: "My job was to speak at Northwestern. *Your* job is to figure out how the message connects back in your hometown in Kentucky." How else to have a nation of interfaith preachers unless they practice the song?

# PART III

# COLLEGES

I squared my shoulders, folded my arms, did my best to look fierce, and crossed the line. My friend Chris's eyes grew wide as he watched me. It was a "Wow, that's something I didn't know about Eboo" expression. It's what I was aiming for. We were juniors and seniors, campus-leader types at the University of Illinois, going through a two-week resident-adviser training at the end of which, the theory was, we would be prepared to take responsibility for fifty to sixty younger students, mostly freshmen. We had a session on supporting students who were struggling academically, a workshop dealing with roommate conflict, and some training on identifying symptoms of depression, but a good half of our time was given over to diversity issues. Crossing the line was a typical exercise. The facilitator would read out a question that was meant to allow the people of color an opportunity to share their experience of being dark in America and to teach the white people in the room a thing or two: "Cross the line if you ever wanted blue eyes." "Cross the line if you were embarrassed by the smell of the food your parents cooked at home." "Cross the line if you wanted to change your name so that it sounded more American." Most of the questions resulted in the people of color doing a lot of the moving—crossing to the other side with somewhat defiant "Yeah, I went through this" looks—and a group of white people shifting uncomfortably in place, looking helpless and forlorn.

I loved crossing the line. I loved diversity training. I loved the phrase "person of color." I loved the helpless looks on the faces of white people when we did multicultural activities. Growing up in the white western suburbs of Chicago, I was ashamed of my skin, my name, my mother's name, my mother's accent, my mother country. At the University of Illinois, I felt like I had entered a magic kingdom where the most powerful spell was role reversal. Those of us who had grown up on the margins were now at the center. Those who had known only the center were now on the sidelines, required to watch as the others were given the stage to tell our stories. I was no longer the dorky brown kid who got picked last for kickball games. I was now in the spotlight holding a microphone, with permission to roar.

My campus in the mid-1990s, like just about every other campus in the country, was in the swing of multiculturalism. You couldn't walk ten feet in any direction without running into somebody reading Cornel West's *Race Matters* or hearing a heated debate about black women's role in the feminist movement. Just a few years earlier, multiculturalism was an abstract theory being discussed in the seminar rooms of the humanities building. Now, it was a full-fledged movement that impacted every corner of the campus.

No incident was more responsible for that shift than the beating of black motorist Rodney King by four white Los Angeles Police Department officers in 1991. Actually, it was more like a series of nightmarish events than a single incident. The officers used a Taser on King, hit him fifty-six times with a baton, focusing especially on his joints, then kicked him six times for good measure. The incident was caught on camera by a private citizen—something almost unheard of back then—and the footage was broadcast around the clock and around the world. The following year, a jury with not a single black member acquitted the four officers. That judgment sparked off riots in Los Angeles that lasted several days and claimed over fifty lives. On the third day, Rodney King appeared on television and appealed for peace: "Please, we can get along here. We all can get along. I mean, we're all stuck here for a while. Let's try to work it out. Let's try to beat it. Let's try to beat it. Let's try to work it out." It was the icing on the cake: the black victim of the brutal beating by four white police officers was calling for reconciliation, not revenge. Even President George H. W. Bush, who had been accused of cynically playing the race card himself in a campaign commercial featuring a black criminal named Willie Horton, said he was "stunned" by the verdict.

For advocates of multiculturalism on college campuses, the events around the Rodney King incident were a case study in American racism. At the center of the problem were profound differences in power and profoundly warped perceptions. Simply put, white people's privilege put them in positions like that of police officer and juror, and their prejudice caused them to use that power oppressively. The issue in the Rodney King case wasn't just the fact of the beating and the acquittal of the officers; it was the whispers that *maybe Rodney King deserved it.* The thinking went something like this: He might have been unarmed, but that didn't mean he wasn't dangerous. Weren't those white police officers justified in feeling threatened? Didn't they have a right to defend themselves? Especially after they pulled over a speeding car and discovered the driver was . . . *black.* Where I was from, there were pockets where those whispers weren't so soft. At a backyard barbeque, I heard a friend's parent say with pride that if he had been one of the cops, he would have done exactly the same thing. Hell, he would have called in reinforcements just in case. After all, the guy was . . . He didn't have to say it. Everybody knew what he meant.

What did those white cops see in Rodney King's black skin? What do most white Americans see when they see black skin? For those of us who grew up where I did when I did, most of the black people we saw were either dancing in music videos, dunking on the basketball court, or glaring at us in mug shots on the evening news. And if those musicians and those athletes weren't blessed with their unique gifts, chances are, they would have wound up in one of those mug shots on the evening news, too. In other words, when we saw black skin, we thought "threat." I cringe every time I remember what I did in that backyard-barbecue discussion about Rodney King, nodded along with everyone else, hoping that my actions would override my skin color, put me at the center instead of keeping me on the margins.

Thirty years after the civil rights movement, the challenges related to race in America—the power differences, the warped perceptions—persisted. Higher education, to its everlasting credit, recognized this and took on the challenge. College campuses effectively transformed themselves at every level to take race seriously. Affirmative action programs were expanded, increasing the number of students of color on campuses. Establishing a welcoming environment became an overriding priority in student affairs, meaning that freshman-orientation programs and resident-adviser training started to emphasize diversity. The importance of engaging the color line was signaled from every corner of the campus. I remember the football coach at the University of Illinois speaking about how, to build interracial camaraderie on his squad, he had black and white players room together. (At a sports-crazed school like Illinois, messages from the football coach mattered a great deal.) The change was felt on the academic side as well. Minority professors were hired, new courses were added, and Non-Western Civilization and Minority Cultures in America were no longer elective categories; they were now requirements for graduation. Thinking back, every single class that I took in the social sciences or humanities (my areas of concentration) had diversity as a central theme. It was clear that priority around diversity was felt at the very top of the university ladder. When the president of the University of Illinois system met with student leaders at the Urbana campus in 1996, he talked about the importance of science and technology, areas that Illinois emphasized and excelled in. But he also spoke passionately about diversity. He said that to be educated in late-twentieth-century America meant knowing something about minority cultures, having positive and substantive experiences with racial diversity, and having the skills to lead a diverse team. He wanted these to be hallmarks of an Illinois education. In fact, when he shook the hand of a graduate of the University of Illinois, he wanted to feel confident that during her time at Illinois, she had acquired multicultural literacy, experienced multicultural community, and engaged in opportunities in multicultural leadership.

The rationale for colleges to take race seriously was not simply about the campus; it was also an attempt by the higher-education sector to have a positive impact on the broader society. In a culture with continuing tensions between racial and ethnic communities, campuses are a unique place where people from different racial backgrounds can come together, commit themselves to a multicultural agenda, develop an appreciation for cultural narratives that are poorly represented in high school textbooks and in the media, and nurture relationships between people from different backgrounds. Colleges develop a society's leaders and set a country's intellectual and cultural agenda, meaning that the attitudes and relationships nurtured on American campuses impact diversity issues in the broader society. Essentially, the center of the multicultural movement was about renewing the idea that America is about people from different backgrounds coming together to build a nation. To do that, people need open attitudes, appreciative knowledge, and meaningful multicultural relationships. College provides the perfect environment to cultivate all three.

Like any movement, multiculturalism had its fringe. It was a place I knew well. Let's put it this way: I crossed the line a lot. "Cross the line if you asked members of your family not to speak their native language in public." "Cross the line if you have ever wished you were white." I was always moving— proudly, passionately, frequently. The next question: "Cross the line if, when you are just hanging out with your friends, people mistake you for being in a gang." That's the one that provoked the extra-hard look from me, and the extra-wide eyes from Chris. I came back and stood next to him, arms still folded, eyes still locked in a fierce glare. Chris leaned in to whisper something to me. I thought he was going to tell me how enriched he felt by this exercise, how appreciative he was to learn this new layer in my life. Instead, he said, "Dude, you're an Indian kid, *from Glen Ellyn.* I could understand you being frustrated if people stereotyped you as an engineering student or they asked you to fix their computer or something. But being in a gang? *Give me a fucking break.*"

The center of the multicultural movement may have been about advancing the American project, but the fringe was characterized by all kinds of excess. There was the ludicrous belief that the only people with interesting stories to tell were people of color, and that the most interesting parts of those stories were the parts about being oppressed. It meant that people woke up in the morning looking for ways that they were marginalized, and if they couldn't find any, inventing them. I spent a lot of time seeking and inventing. I remember being fifteen minutes late for a noon lunch appointment with a white friend, and when he looked impatiently at his watch as I sat down with my tray, I snapped that I refused to be colonized by his white notions of time. "Eboo," he said, trying to keep his voice even, "we both have one o'clock classes. Your being late isn't about you being oppressed; it's about us having less time for lunch together."

As much as I liked lecturing my white friends on campus about identity politics, I focused most of my energy on a certain unsuspecting middle-aged Indian who had immigrated to America two decades earlier. Once or twice during a semester, I would pack my dirty laundry in the back of my parents' Oldsmobile and drive north on I-57 for a home-cooked meal and another opportunity to educate my dad, practicing my lecture out loud on the way. Why had he told me to read John Steinbeck and Ken Kesey growing up? Why not Richard Wright or Ralph Ellison—were they too radical

for his suburban tastes because they were *black?* (Clearly, I
didn't pay attention to Steinbeck and Kesey if I didn't think
they were radical, he told me.) My father lay languidly on
the sofa, watching football (exploitation of minority athletes,
I told him), regarding the fruit of his tuition dollars with
mild curiosity, raising his eyebrows when I said something
that he thought crossed the line, occasionally intervening
when he thought I was edging close to the cliff.

"You're lecturing me as if I know nothing about being
a minority," he told me during halftime of one Bears game.
"I was one of the only brown students at Notre Dame in the
mid-1970s, I was one of an even smaller number of brown
guys to be an executive in corporate advertising, and I was
one of the first brown people to start a business in the village
of Lisle, so stop acting as if you own all things brown."

"Plus," he said, "for all your talk about identity, you have
never once mentioned the dimension of identity driving
world affairs."

I was about to say something self-righteous when he interrupted with a phrase that felt out of left field: "Religious
identity, Eboo. Religious identity. That's what people are
killing each other over these days. If you don't believe me,
just look at the newspaper. Listen, the next time you want
to act like the world's expert on diversity, please first tell me
how you plan to solve religious conflict." The second half had
just started; he turned back to the game. I left in a huff, my
folded laundry and Tupperware containers of home-cooked
food in the back seat of the Olds. Clearly, my dad had been
so thoroughly assimilated that his only response to my at-
tempts to raise his consciousness was to try to divert me.

A few weeks later, a friend of mine called, choking back
sobs, and said, "Did you hear the news? Yitzhak Rabin was
assassinated."

Looking back, the headlines of the 1990s read like a narrative of religious conflict: There was the 1993 bombing of
the World Trade Center, announcing the global ambitions
of Muslim extremism. There was the war in the Balkans,

where Slobodan Milosevic's soldiers held up three fingers for the Trinity as they launched their mortars into the majority-Muslim and nearly defenseless city of Sarajevo. A half century earlier, a Hindu nationalist in India had assassinated Mahatma Gandhi. In the 1990s, political parties affiliated with the group the assassin belonged to roared back to power in India, winning the election in 1998 and promptly testing a nuclear weapon, which they called "the Hindu bomb." An explosion went off at the 1996 Olympics in Atlanta, and Eric Rudolph held up the Bible as his inspiration. A few years later, Benjamin Smith chose the Fourth of July weekend to go on a shooting spree across Illinois and Indiana, targeting Jews, blacks, and Asians, motivated by the racist theology of the World Church of the Creator. When Yitzhak Rabin's assassin appeared in an Israeli court, he proudly stated that the murder was rooted in Jewish scripture and law. When asked if he acted alone, he replied, "It was God."[1]

We were too busy reading critical race theory to pay attention to any of this. The problem of the color line blinded us to the coming challenge of the faith line. We even ignored the religious dimensions of obvious issues. We talked a lot about Cornel West the Black Panther, and not at all about Cornel West the black Baptist. We viewed the university's mascot, Chief Illiniwek, as a racist symbol but knew almost nothing about the spiritual role that chiefs played in Native American religious culture. And for all our talk about the importance of identity, of the personal being political, of knowing one another's stories, we knew almost nothing about each other's religious lives.

Every other Monday night, we resident advisers would gather for additional training. Diversity was again a centerpiece, but because time was shorter, these were generally more straightforward discussions with fewer crossing-the-line-type exercises. One Monday night, the question we were told to answer was "Tell us about a time when you felt marginalized based on your identity." The white kids knew their part:

"I'll pass. I just want to listen and learn from the experience of those who are oppressed."

My friend Hussein's turn came up. He started slowly: "So, last week, in the dining hall, a group of older students, including some resident advisers, were part of something they called a Viking Dinner. They got mashed potatoes, peas, and chicken from the food line, came back to their table, and basically smooshed their food on each other's heads and bodies and made loud grunting sounds."

The other resident advisers started to smirk, me with them. We'd all seen this, and as Hussein said, some of us had participated. It was messy, it was funny, it was a break from the normal routine. Hussein waited for the chortling to die down. He had no look of defiance on his face, but he wanted to get through his story: "I couldn't sit there and watch it," he said. "I packed my food up and left and finished my dinner in my room alone. The whole thing just made me really uncomfortable. Actually, I couldn't stop thinking about it, and the more I did, the more I realized that I was more than uncomfortable, I was offended."

The smirks were slowly evaporating now. People were looking at Hussein with some concern. We were remembering we were resident advisers, not Vikings. We did not want one of our own—a brown fellow, no less—to feel offended. We leaned in; we wanted to know more. Hussein continued. "Where I come from, food is life, and life is precious—it's from God. That's what we are taught in Islam."

The facial expressions started to change. They weren't looks of concern anymore; they were more like those of confusion. If Hussein had said he was offended because he was Indian, he would have gotten sympathetic head nods. Nationality and ethnicity were part of our diversity radar. If Hussein said he didn't like the Viking dinner because Vikings oppressed gay people, he might have gotten a hug. Every year I had been in college, sexual orientation had become a larger part of diversity training. But hearing that he was offended because of a religious sensibility was confusing. People weren't hostile to it; they just didn't know what to do with it. They had no framework. It simply didn't register.

A few nights later, as I was walking through the third floor of my dorm, I heard the sound of an acoustic guitar and a chorus of sweet-sounding voices. The door was ajar, and I peeked inside. It was Allen Hall's InterVarsity Christian Fellowship group, holding a prayer circle. I saw a friend from class in the room, met her eyes, and exchanged a smile. I stood at the door and listened for a moment as they sang, "Lord, I Lift Your Name on High." As I walked to the stairs, I realized that this was a regular occurrence. I had passed that room dozens of times before, seen people slip inside and take a seat in the circle, heard the faint echoes of soft songs coming through the door. Half the time, I was off to some meeting or lecture about identity. The Latino students were preparing to meet a senior university administrator to insist that, as their cultural center got remodeled, the mural be saved. Asian American students were agitating for their own cultural center, African American students wanted more black faculty hires, women were discussing whether men could be part of the Take Back the Night march. I was immersed in several such discourses and had become a strong advocate for many of those causes. I believed that *identity matters.*

But what of this other identity that we activist types talked so little about? This identity that my friend Hussein spoke of, the one that drew thousands of students at the University of Illinois into prayer circles on a regular basis, the dimension of people's lives that—my father had it right—was driving world affairs?

In the early 2000s, a family friend who was a student at the University of Illinois visited me at Interfaith Youth Core's offices on the near North Side of Chicago. I got the scoop on my old coffee and pizza haunts down in Champaign-Urbana, and then I asked about the campus activist scene. "It's all about identity," she told me. "Same as when I was in college," I retorted. "What's the latest?"

She told me about how different student groups were bringing in fiery speakers they knew would make inflammatory statements and offend other groups. Those groups would respond by bringing in their own fiery and offensive speakers, continuing the cycle. There were demonstrations and counterdemonstrations, ugly and accusatory op-eds and letters were flying back and forth in the *Daily Illini,* students from different groups were chalking the quad with demeaning slurs directed at one another. It had gotten so heated that worried parents were calling university administrators, who, frankly, didn't know what to do. It sounded uglier than any of the ethnic or racial tensions I witnessed when I was a student. I wondered if something had gone awry with the Asian American activist movement that had started in the 1990s. "Who are the groups involved?" I asked, a little nervous to hear the response. The answer could not have surprised me more: "Mostly Jews and Muslims," she said. "It's stuff related to the Middle East." The headlines in world affairs were starting to draw the fault lines on college campuses.[2]

As I talked with my contacts down in Champaign, I realized that campus politics related to the Middle East was just one religious tension point among many. After George W. Bush's victory over Al Gore in the 2000 election, which the dominant media narrative credited to the resurgent power of Evangelicals in America, Christians on campus felt harassed in classrooms and residence halls. Mel Gibson's film *The Passion of the Christ* had deeply offended Jewish groups, who pointed out that the characters who sent Jesus to the cross looked like Jews out of some early-twentieth-century anti-Semite's imagination. And, of course, the shadow of 9/11 loomed over everything. A decade earlier, my resident adviser friend Hussein's religious identity had been somewhere between invisible and a mystery to most people. In the early 2000s, Muslim students felt anything but invisible or mysterious. They felt immediately marked

and explicitly labeled, like they wore a scarlet letter *E,* for
*enemy.*

I remember sitting in the student center of a midsize college in a midsize Midwestern city, making final preparations
for a talk I was giving there and looking up to see a woman
wearing a headscarf walk by a flat-screen TV playing cable
news. I saw a couple of students sitting at a table, finishing
dinner, watching a story about Muslim terrorism. There
were the stock images of angry Muslims with beards pumping their fists and burning American flags, and the news-
caster said something about a spike in the number of suicide
bombings. One of the students nodded in the direction of
the unsuspecting Muslim woman, pointed to the television,
and said to his friend, "Maybe they're related." They both
laughed and went back to their dinner.

I was furious. I got up, all ready to give them a piece of
my mind on discrimination. And then I caught myself. That
was me, in high school, when it came to race. What set me
straight was college.

What did those students at that Midwestern college see
when they looked at that Muslim woman? What do many
people see when they look at Evangelicals or Mormons or
Buddhists or Catholics or Jews—or atheists, for that matter?
Where do they get that information? Do they have knowledge or relationships that challenge the stereotypes presented by Hollywood or the evening news? And what is their
campus doing to advance an alternative narrative, teach an
appreciative knowledge base, create spaces for meaningful
relationships, offer opportunities for leadership, provide a
model for the rest of the society *on interfaith issues?*

Starting in the 1980s and 1990s, a small group of college
professors and campus chaplains started to give voice to this
agenda. Harvard professor Diana Eck wrote in *Encountering
God* that *religion* was the missing word in the diversity discussion.[3] Sandy and Helen Astin, at the University of California
at Los Angeles, published research suggesting that under-

grads came to college seeking conversations about religion and spirituality but were frequently disappointed at the lack of them.[4] Chaplains like Janet Cooper Nelson, Sharon Kugler, and Scotty McLennan started cocurricular programs that filled this gap. These multifaith councils and interfaith discussion dinners became the place that interested undergrads came to talk about their religious identities and spiritual journeys. Victor Kazanjian, the chaplain at Wellesley College, not only started programs on his own campus but also a national network called Education as Transformation, which publishes resources and organizes conferences on religious diversity and spirituality.

Important as these programs are, they tend to be at private schools on the East Coast, the type of college that can afford to hire part-time Hindu and Buddhist leaders to minister to a few dozen religious-minority students. The programs occupy an important niche—interested students at elite schools. The big question for interfaith cooperation in higher ed, however, is how to go from niche to norm, just like the multicultural movement did. From private institutions on the coasts to public universities in the Midwest, from the small group of students who actively seek out such programs to part of the orientation for incoming freshmen and the required training for resident advisers. To go from niche to norm, you'd need everyone from presidents to professors to chaplains to students to view this work as a high priority, something to be not just talked about but also acted on, and to be not just done but also done well.

One of the victories of the multicultural movement was to make it standard practice for campuses to survey their students on attitudes, knowledge, and relationships related to race, ethnicity, and sexuality. Why not administer a religious-diversity survey asking the same questions about Muslims, Mormons, Evangelicals, and atheists? Today, a student can major in sociology and get a concentration in race, class, and gender. Why not have the possibility of majoring in religion and taking a sequence of courses that would qualify for a concentration in interfaith leadership? Without a doubt, the external impetus exists. If the Rodney King incident and its aftermath raised the volume on race relations in our society, prompting campuses to take on the challenge, certainly 9/11 and its various effects have had a similar impact when it comes to interfaith issues.

Every year, colleges inject a stream of impassioned, idealistic new leaders into our nation who are itching to take on our toughest challenges. They bring with them the knowledge and relationships, the attitudes and skills, they learned on campus. Those of us who went to college in the 1990s could easily be called the Multicultural Leadership Generation. After we graduated, we started diversity groups in our cities and our companies and pushed Hollywood and major retailers to diversify representation. We wanted to bring our values to the highest stage possible, so when Barack Obama announced his candidacy for president of the United States of America, we worked day and night to help elect a man who combined genes from Kenya and Kansas, who grew up in Hawaii and Indonesia, who worked as a community organizer on the South Side of Chicago and was the first black president of the *Harvard Law Review.*

What if colleges took religious diversity as seriously as they took other identity issues? What if recruiting a religiously diverse student body, creating a welcoming environment for people of different faiths and philosophical perspectives, and offering classes in interfaith studies and co-curricular opportunities for interfaith community and leadership became the norm? What if university presidents expected their graduates to acquire interfaith literacy, experience interfaith community, and have opportunities to run interfaith programs during their four years on campus? What impact might a critical mass of interfaith leaders have on America over the course of the next generation?

There is certainly no lack of interest among students. Every year at Interfaith Youth Core we raise the number of students we expect at our Interfaith Leadership Institutes, and every year we still find ourselves scrambling at the last minute to accommodate all the interest. For all the mistakes we've made at Interfaith Youth Core, our basic instinct was right on. Young people don't like to have their own faiths or the faiths of their friends maligned. They don't view people from different faiths in an inevitable clash of civilizations. They desperately want a vocabulary that helps them stay grounded in their own tradition and relate positively to those from other traditions. The more they see religious bomb throwers, the more committed they are to being interfaith bridge builders.

Greg Damhorst is a prime example. Greg grew up in Elgin, a middle-class suburb about forty miles northwest of Chicago. The Evangelical church he attended was right next to his diverse high school, and because of the way the roads were configured, parking at the church was easier than parking at the school. This concerned some church members, who felt that the church parking lot was private property that should be used only by church members. A group showed up one morning and strung a rope across the entrance. If you were a member of the church, they lowered the rope and let you in. If you weren't, well, then you had to turn around and find a different place to park.

Greg is the type of guy for whom ropes across his church parking lot raise deep theological questions. One of Greg's high school friends was a young man from a Hindu background, and Greg couldn't help but think about him every time he parked at church and walked across the lot to school. Was this how Christians were supposed to invite people to Jesus? It felt a little like a Jesus tollbooth: put the right coins in and the gate would lift. What if someone said yes, he was interested in the church but only because he wanted to park in the lot? What if someone else who truly could be seeking Jesus was turned off by the rope?

Greg brought these questions with him to the University of Illinois. He believed deeply in his faith—indeed, believed it was the only way to God. He also believed that the best way to express his faith, to walk in the footsteps of Jesus, was to be in right relationship with the world, including people of other faiths. Right relationship means respect, understanding, and cooperation. So, in addition to being part of an Evangelical Christian association, Greg joined the Interfaith in Action student group (set up by a group of Illinois students who spent a summer interning at Interfaith Youth Core) and quickly became a leader in its weekly shared-values discussion and annual Day of Interfaith Service. On a good day, twenty students came to the discussion. Interfaith in Action could expect 120 or so for the annual service day, when Interfaith in Action leaders organized students into religiously diverse groups for a day of volunteering and then facilitated small-group discussions about the shared value of service across faiths.

The numbers remained modest for several years, but the network of relationships that Interfaith in Action cultivated were increasingly impressive. Directors of local social-service agencies came to respect Greg and his colleagues and to rely on the annual volunteer day. Campus officials, including the vice chancellor, learned about their work. The leaders of various religious student organizations encouraged their members to participate in the discussions and the days of service, resulting in markedly lower tension between religious communities across the campus. Personally, Greg felt fulfilled. The model of discussing shared values like mercy and compassion with people of different traditions and applying those values in interfaith service projects allowed him to speak openly about his Christian inspiration while also listening respectfully to others.

In January 2010, a catastrophic earthquake hit Haiti, killing tens of thousands of people and leaving a million homeless. Greg and the Interfaith in Action's executive committee started to organize. They found the most practical way they could help: packing nutritious dry-goods meals. And they set a goal: the University of Illinois and the Champaign-Urbana community would pack a million meals for Haiti in a weekend. Directors of local social-service agencies helped them find a space large enough for the event. One helped them get a federal grant to pay for the food and materials. They mobilized their network among student and community religious communities. They pasted butcher paper on a wall so that people could write what inspired them to serve. In a twelve-hour period, over five thousand people packaged over a million meals for Haiti. Hundreds took the time to leave a quote about service from their tradition on the wall.

This story is a perfect illustration of why college campuses are an ideal civic laboratory for interfaith cooperation. All the positive social capital in our broader society—faith-based groups, volunteer programs, educational opportunities, forums for discussion and exchange—exist on campuses in concentrated form. Students like Greg can go to a gathering of their Evangelical Christian group at 6 p.m., walk across the hall to a session of their interfaith club at 7:30 p.m., notice that that the theme of both meetings is faith and service, and drop by the room of their resident adviser at 9 p.m. to ask for help in planning a panel discussion on the subject. The key leaders can meet the next morning for breakfast and start to put the program together. A professor of Islamic studies, a Jewish faculty member from the theater department, and an Evangelical Christian who teaches chemistry might be the invited panelists for a discussion on how faith inspires service across traditions. Perhaps the college's secular-humanist volunteer coordinator attends the program and says that she knows a Catholic church in the community that has just opened up a homeless shelter and is looking for volunteers.

If the audience assembled here wanted to apply the value of service in a real-world interfaith project, this is an ideal opportunity. All of this can happen relatively quickly and easily on a campus, all stemming from the flash insight of a student and encouraged along by the professionals on a campus whose job it is to nurture student leadership. The most critical factor in nurturing young leaders is giving them a place to apply their leadership skills, to form an idea, and to make it a reality. Campuses pride themselves in being that space. If Greg and his group hadn't run several interfaith service projects with a hundred students, there is no way they could have run a program with five thousand.

I excitedly told Greg that he was putting all the theories into practice—bringing people from a range of backgrounds together in common projects, bridging social capital, turning diversity into pluralism, creating networks of engagement, working the interfaith triangle. Greg stopped me. He was happy about all that, but he had done this in the name of a different philosopher. Greg quoted him: "I was hungry, and you brought me something to eat."

This issue is personal for students, part of their core. And when something becomes personal for students, it quickly becomes personal for faculty, staff, and administrators across college campuses.

Per Tarek Elmasry's advice, Interfaith Youth Core had narrowed its focus to higher education. No more traipsing off to Kazakhstan when the State Department called; our staff now spent most of its time on college campuses. I personally visit about twenty-five campuses per year, giving keynote talks on interfaith cooperation and speaking with faculty, administrators, and students about making interfaith a priority. The range of responses I've gotten is an interesting illustration of where the movement is at.

When I suggested to a group of graduate students in higher education at a public university in the Deep South (people who would one day be vice chancellors of student affairs) that they become literate in religious diversity, one raised his hand and said to me point blank, "We don't talk about religion here." At a conference of student-affairs administrators, someone stood up and said she was a lesbian and that religion had been nothing but a force of oppression in her life. At Chicago's DePaul University, the nation's largest Catholic higher-ed institution and among the most diverse, a staff member mentioned to me off-handedly, "We love religious diversity, even though wc arc Catholic." At Bcrca College, a Christian liberal arts school in Kentucky, a minister at the chapel where I was to give my keynote address asked if I would be more comfortable if he put a blanket over the large cross that hung behind the podium.

Frankly, I expected to encounter more hostility when I started talking about higher education making interfaith cooperation a priority. After all, high-profile aggressive atheists like Daniel Dennett and Richard Dawkins, who call universities home, delight in wielding traditional academic values (reason, science) like a bludgeon against religion. I would characterize the sentiment that I've come across as discomfort rather than hostility, a discomfort largely borne from a lack of knowledge. If you work in student affairs and part of your role is to create a welcoming environment for gay students and your formative experiences with religion are Christians from the small town where you grew up speaking negatively about gay people, then it makes sense that you see faith as a problem. "Does it ever happen," I asked the student-affairs administrator who told me religion is hostile to homosexuality, "that you have a student from another country or from a minority community—say, black or Latino—who says that being gay is against thcir culturc?"

"Sure," she responded. "My job is to talk with thcm. I tcll them about the heroes of their culture who were gay that they might not know about. I point them to writers from their own backgrounds who have a more progressive perspective than the ones they have been exposed to. The goal is to show them that welcoming people who are different is actually a part of their culture."

"So why not use the same approach when it comes to religion and homosexuality?" I asked. "Why not point Christians who might have qualms with homosexuality to gay faith heroes in their own tradition, or to Christian theologies of welcoming?"

"I guess I just don't know that territory very well," she responded.

"You could start with Peter Gomes," I suggested. Gomes,

who died a few years ago, was the minister of Harvard's Memorial Church, an openly gay African American clergyman
who preached around the world, offered prayers at the inau-
gurations of two Republican presidents, and wrote a stack of
widely respected books on Christianity.

Higher-education officials have spent years reading
widely and deeply in the literature of multiculturalism, and
so feel equipped to deal with the normal culture conflicts
that emerge during those conversations. They have little or
no fluency in interfaith matters. This is a solvable problem.
Consider the fact that race, gender, class, and sexuality are
equally complex issues. The reason we have a robust movement devoted to these issues is because people within the
academy decided they were important enough to soldier
through all the challenges and address. Religious diversity
requires the same time, effort, and purpose.

The graduate student at the public university in the Deep
South seemed to think that faith doesn't belong in public life
at all, and definitely not in higher education. "Really?" I responded. "I've been flipping channels in my hotel room and
it seems like every other person on your local television station wants to talk about religion, and much of what they have
to say belittles much of what you value. Let's get something
straight: just because you are not talking about religion in
graduate school does not mean that religion is not getting
talked about. It just means you are forfeiting the conversation to someone else." Part of the responsibility of public universities is to prepare citizens for engaged life in America,
an America that is now among the most religiously diverse
nations in human history. As the Truman Commission on
Higher Education wrote in 1947, "The first and most essential
charge of higher education is that at all levels and in all its
fields of specialization, it shall be the carrier of democratic
values, ideals, and process."[5]

When I shared with the president of DePaul University
his staffer's comment that they love people of other religions
even though they are Catholic, he laughed and said, "My goal

is to help build a campus culture where people say, 'We love religious diversity *because* we're Catholic.'" This highlights the interesting challenge that religious colleges face. There are many such institutions, obvious ones like the Evangelical Wheaton College and less obvious ones like the University of Chicago (started by Baptists) and most of the Ivy League schools. In fact, two-thirds of the colleges that are part of the Council of Independent Colleges, one of the larger higher-education networks in the country, have some sort of religious affiliation. In many cases, as with Ivy League schools, it means that religious communities played some role in the founding of the institution. In other cases, as with Catholic, Lutheran, and Evangelical schools, those colleges view part of their mission as advancing a religious influence. These schools almost always have strong religion departments and some type of religion requirement.

So, how does a religiously affiliated college live out its heritage and identity in a world characterized by religious diversity, when even its student body comes from many different backgrounds? That's what the staff person at Berea's chapel was struggling with. His offer to cover the cross was a gesture of hospitality, an attempt to make a Muslim guest comfortable at the Christian college.

Berea is a special place. Located in the foothills of the Appalachian Mountains, it was founded by an abolitionist named John G. Fee who was committed to building an institution that lived out the biblical line "God has made of one blood all the peoples of the earth."[6] In that vein, Berea started as a school where blacks and whites, men and women, studied together. That was nothing short of radical for Kentucky in the 1850s. Today, that vision expresses itself in an institution where there are basically two requirements for entry: you have to be academically promising and you have to be poor. Berea charges no tuition. Every student works on campus at least ten hours a week so that the college can simply function. And in addition to being racially diverse, Berea is becoming increasingly religiously diverse as well, a fact that led them to bring me, a Muslim speaker, to campus.

I considered that history as I looked at the cross and I thought to myself, "That cross is why this college exists. John Fee risked his life to build an institution that brought people from different backgrounds together.[7] I'm standing here, a Muslim interfaith leader, because Berea believes that cross signifies an inclusive and relational Christian identity. I don't want them to cover the cross. I don't want them to hide their Christian faith. I want them to tell the story of how that cross inspired them to build an interracial college in pre–Civil War Kentucky. I want them to share how that cross moves them to admit Buddhists from Sri Lanka and Hindus from India and have them in classes and volunteer activities with Christians from Appalachia. I want them to tell the world, 'This is what it means to be Christian.' "

What *does* it mean to be Christian in a world of people of different faith backgrounds? It's a question that seminaries and divinity schools wrestle with just as much as religious colleges do. These institutions, though smaller in number and size than undergraduate campuses, will play an out-size role in America's interfaith future. They train religious leaders, they advance new theological understandings, and they send signals that point the way for denominations and congregations. We have partnered with seminaries from the beginning at IFYC, teaching classes, designing youth theology programs, and being part of continuing education for ministers. The issues being discussed in seminaries today will shape the identities of people of faith for generations to come.

# SEMINARIES

It was the Muslims who brought the various communities of Christians together. Blacks, whites, and Latinos, some long-time residents and others recent immigrants, groups that had long eyed one another with suspicion on the factory floors and small-town streets of Grand Island, Nebraska, were now lining up shoulder to shoulder together, their collective anger directed at the recent arrivals.

"The Latino is very humble," said Raul Garcia, a Mexican American who had immigrated in 1994, "but they are arrogant. They act like the United States owes them." Margaret Hornady, a white woman and Grand Island's mayor, said she found the sight of Muslim headscarves "startling." It made her think of Osama bin Laden.

Grand Island is a town of about 50,000 in the southern part of Nebraska, founded in the mid-nineteenth century by German immigrants. It is home to a meat- and poultry-packing plant owned by Swift & Company, the source of much of the employment in the area. To keep up with production demand, the company has recruited recent immigrant groups as labor. Mexicans, Laotians, and Sudanese have all come, worked in the plant, and settled down in the area. Such factories are frequently targeted for immigration raids, and one such raid gutted the labor force of the Grand Island plant. Management decided it no longer paid to recruit workers who were potentially in the United States illegally. They came up with a solution: recruit immigrant workers who have political refugee status, and with it legal papers. Minnesota had a large number of these in the form of Somalis, an immigrant group who also happened to be Muslim.

For the most part, the Somali Muslims were fine with doing their daily prayers during lunch and bathroom breaks. But during the month of Ramadan, they requested a special quitting time so they could properly prepare to perform the more elaborate rituals that surrounded ending the fast. That would disrupt production at the plant, management responded. Many of the Somalis complained bitterly; a few dozen actually quit. Finally, a compromise was reached—everybody would get their dinner break at that time. That meant a shorter workday by fifteen minutes, which meant fifteen minutes less pay. The Muslims were happy with this; it was a sacrifice they were more than willing to make for their faith. But it was too much for the black, white, and Latino workers, many of whom felt the Somali Muslims had been requesting special privileges since they arrived. First, it was about getting Muslim holidays off, then it was about not handling pork products on the production line. Rumors were flying that Somalis had received pay raises while everyone else was getting a pay cut. The frustration boiled over. A thousand workers walked out together.

Here is your assignment, I told my class at Chicago's McCormick Theological Seminary: Imagine you were serving a church in Grand Island, Nebraska, when these events took place. A *New York Times* reporter calls you and asks for your comment on the situation as a pastor. What do you say?

One student questioned the relevance: Grand Island had to be an exception. She'd grown up in a small town in Nebraska, and there were no Latino Catholics—forget Somali Muslims—for many miles in any direction. America was changing, I assured her. A version of what played out in Grand Island had also occurred in Shelbyville, Tennessee; Greeley, Colorado; Postville, Iowa; and more than a dozen other such towns across America. Whatever church she served after she graduated from seminary, whether it was located in a small town or a big city, there was a pretty good chance she'd be dealing with religious diversity.

A furious discussion ensued. One person said that because America needs economic growth, it was a bad idea for the Muslims to be given special time off for prayers. The factory would be less productive if it had to close fifteen minutes early. Another was aghast: America was built on religious freedom, she insisted. It's why the Pilgrims came; it's what the First Amendment is about. What about the rights of the other workers to make a decent wage? a third student asked. People took sides and argued passionately: capitalism versus the Constitution, economic productivity versus religious freedom, faith identity versus class identity.

I was following each turn of the conversation closely, fascinated by the breadth of issues my students were raising. My IFYC colleague and co-teacher Cassie had a different reaction. She'd earned a master's degree in divinity at the University of Chicago before joining our staff and viewed the debate through the perspective of a Christian leader herself. What she saw was a room full of future members of the clergy whose assignment was to imagine they were serving in a town experiencing religious tension and to comment on the situation as Christian leaders. In the thirty minutes of debate, nobody had quoted Scripture, nobody had asked what Jesus would do, nobody had referenced the example of Christian leaders in similar situations. As seminary students, they were immersed in learning the religious language of the Christian tradition, but when asked to apply it to a situation of interfaith conflict, they avoided Christian language completely and defaulted to other modes. Finally, Cassie interrupted the discussion and said, "Remember, you are being asked to comment as a pastor, not as an economist or a constitutional-law professor. What do you have to say about this *as a pastor?*"

There was silence. I could see the wheels turning in people's heads, and I noticed frustration on some faces. Finally, someone said, "What difference can a pastor make in this situation, anyway?" It was a perfect opportunity to present our next case study.

Jersey City, New Jersey, has the largest concentration of Egyptian Americans in the country—about 50,000 total, roughly half Christian and half Muslim. Tensions between the two groups are thick in Egypt, but in Jersey City, for the most part, they have gotten along just fine. Kids play football together in neighborhood parks, adults go into business together, twentysomethings share *shisha* pipes in hip cafés.[1]

In January 2005, there was a heinous murder of an Egyptian Christian family—four people found bound, gagged, and stabbed to death. It was a crime that tore the Egyptian Christians and Muslims of Jersey City apart. Christian mourners threatened to beat a Muslim sheik who attended the funeral. When Mohsen Elesawi, an Egyptian Muslim limousine driver, walked into his favorite café to share a *shisha* pipe and a game of chess with his Christian friends, they turned away and gave him the cold shoulder. Teenagers from the two communities no longer sat together for lunch at Dickinson High School. "I'm not going to be friends with Muslims anymore—their parents killed my best friend," a student at the high school declared, his eyes welling with tears.

As the tensions grew, the rumors spread. The slain father had been known to engage in theological debates with Muslims, so the killing was obviously a religious revenge job. The daughter had a cross tattooed on her wrist, and the murdering Muslim had driven a knife through it. Such details were not confirmed by the police investigating the murder. In the teeth of the bitter divide, the authorities tried to emphasize a simple fact: This was an unsolved crime.

When the culprit was finally found, it turned out that he was neither Egyptian nor Muslim. The murder was not a religious execution, it was part of a robbery attempt. The best name for the killer was simple: killer.

As our seminary students read through the case, one of them spoke up and said he was confused: "I just don't get it. Here are two communities who get along, who seem to have left old tensions behind and are building a good life together in America. There is no real evidence that this was about religion or that Muslims were involved. It seems to me that this could just as easily have brought Muslims and Christians in Jersey City together instead of driving them apart. So, why didn't it?"

The answer is buried in the middle of the article. A group of leaders who were part of a religious group, the American Coptic Association, called a press conference on the steps of the slain family's church shortly after the murder. Their message was simple and clear: This was a religious execution carried out by Muslims. "Wake up, America!" yelled Dr. Monir Dawoud, the president of the group, during his speech. He and other speakers elaborated: the Muslims had killed these Christians, just like they routinely killed people in the Middle East, just like they killed people on 9/11. When would Christians, America, the world get it? Muslims everywhere were crazy fanatics who had to be stopped.

After my students absorbed that paragraph, I pointed to some lines further down the page: "We never talk about religion," an Egyptian Muslim high school student told Andrea Elliott, the *New York Times* reporter who wrote the article. An Egyptian Christian student agreed: "We don't put religion in our friendship at all."

One of my students raised her hand. "I think I get it now. The faith leaders willing to use religious language were the ones who were framing this situation as Christians versus Muslims. They held their press conference on the steps of a church, and they called this a Muslim execution. The Muslims and Christians who maintained friendships even through the tension, they didn't seem to have the religious language to convey why this ought to be understood as Jersey City versus murderers instead of Christians versus Muslims. Religious language resonates with a lot of people, and if those of us who have a vision of a diverse community

having a common life together don't articulate that vision using religious language, we simply forfeit the cross, the Bible,
even the example of Jesus, to the people who will."

"I wonder what I would preach in church the Sunday after this happened?" another student wondered out loud.

"That," said Cassie, "is your next assignment."

Cassie came to the question of what it means to be a person
of strong faith in a situation of diversity in a very personal
way. When she was a teenager, she devoted her life to Christ.
Her somewhat surprised parents found themselves dropping
their daughter off at a conservative Evangelical church on
Sunday mornings in the suburbs of Seattle, the only region
in the country where more people check "None" than "Christian" on surveys of religiosity. There, Cassie learned Scripture and praise songs, leadership and humility, what it means
to be saved and how to spread the Good News to save others.

When she graduated from high school, Cassie went to
a liberal arts college in Wisconsin. There were only enough
Christians there to form a single student group. It included
mainline Protestants as well as Evangelicals, people whose
idea of worship was sitting stiffly in church pews and others who spoke in tongues. It also included Catholics. This
was something of a challenge for Cassie. In the church where
she was baptized, she had been told that Catholics aren't
Christian.

Soon, Catholics became the least of Cassie's theological worries. During her time as an undergraduate, Cassie
became friends with a young Muslim from Bangladesh.
She found him to be righteous and pious and kind, many of
the qualities that she had at one point associated only with
Evangelical Christians. One evening in the library, Ahmed
asked Cassie if he could interview her. Cassie said sure,
and asked why. It turns out that Ahmed was doing a project
for an anthropology class. He had seen Cassie's Bible and
cross, observed her Wednesday-night prayer group, watched
her go to church on Sunday mornings, noticed the distinct

language with which she talked to her tribe, and had chosen to make an ethnographic inquiry into the exotic life of the American Evangelical Christian.

As she answered the questions, talking about the meaning of the cross and reading aloud passages from the Bible, Cassie had the sudden realization that this anthropology exercise presented her with the opportunity she had been hoping for. She took a deep breath and prepared to make her move. Ahmed beat her to it. Looking Cassie deep in the eyes, he said, "You are such a wonderful person, exactly the person I have been looking to share something with. I would like to tell you about my religion—Islam." And with words eerily similar to the ones Cassie was about to say—*truth, love, faith, God*—Ahmed tried to convert her.

For a second there, Cassie was stunned. She had spent years in church learning the script to convert others, and she now found herself on the receiving end of that process. She wasn't really offended, just surprised. Finally, not really knowing what else to do, she began to blurt out the words that had been gathering in her head since she first met Ahmed: "Has anybody ever told you what it means to have a personal relationship with a man named Jesus?" Now it was Ahmed's turn to be surprised. His eyes got wide, and he started to say something. And then the corners of his mouth started to turn up, and pretty soon they were both laughing.

It is a story that reminds me of the dynamic that the great religious studies scholar and Christian theologian Wilfred Cantwell Smith describes in the introduction to his book *The Faith of Other Men*. As the gender-loaded title suggests, the events the book is based on took place before the midpoint of the twentieth century, when the city of Lahore, where Cantwell Smith was a young professor at a Christian missionary college, was still part of an undivided India under British rule. One day, while going about his normal routine, he had a startling realization about the obvious: most of his colleagues and students at the missionary college were not Christian; they were Sikhs, Muslims, and Hindus. "The Christians among us," he writes, "were attempting to illustrate and practice our faith; our colleagues of other communities, often reverent men, were willing to work with us toward constructing and maintaining a community—a community religiously diverse."[2]

Had he been asked before he arrived what a Christian should do when put in the same room as someone of a different religion, he might well have answered, "Try to convert them." It is, after all, the command of the Great Commission, a central part of the Christian tradition. That desire was no doubt present in him, but when put in a situation where he grew to respect people of other faiths as colleagues and, especially living in an unfamiliar country, rely on them as friends, he found other thoughts arising as well. How were they, together, to most effectively teach their students? What could they do, together, about the increasing religious violence in the subcontinent? What did their religiously diverse community have to say about the colonial regime in place at the time? All these questions, in a community of believers, inevitably became intertwined with faith. For a Christian to think only of converting others in this situation seemed to Cantwell Smith not so much to miss the point as to miss too many other dimensions of life.

Cantwell Smith had no interest in converting to another faith himself, and in a community that worked together and even worshipped with one another, it was facile to believe that all faiths were going to fold into one, or that religion was going to melt away entirely. Ultimately, Cantwell Smith came to this: "The problem is for us all to learn to live together with our seriously different traditions not only in peace but in some sort of mutual trust and mutual loyalty." The question was how to have a vertical relationship with one's own understanding of the divine, and a horizontal relationship with the diversity of the world—in Cantwell Smith's words, to arrive at a point where one "can appreciate other men's values without losing allegiance to our own."

*The Faith of Other Men* was actually written in the early 1960s, some twenty years after Cantwell Smith's experiences in Lahore. By then, he was director of Harvard's Center for the Study of World Religions, and had enough perspective to make some comparative observations. The first was about religious diversity. The United States at that time had just recently started understanding itself as a Judeo-Christian country. It had nowhere near the range of religious diversity that Cantwell Smith had experienced while in Lahore. That would change, he predicted. The diversity of Lahore was on its way to Louisville—air travel, communications technology, and the early emergence of globalization made it inevitable. The kinds of questions he found himself asking at the Christian missionary college in Lahore were the type of questions all believers would soon have to face. As he wrote, "The religious life of mankind from now on, if it is to be lived at all, will be lived in a context of religious pluralism."

Cantwell Smith's second observation had to do with the field of religious studies. Traditionally, comparative religion focused on religious systems—the beliefs, rituals, sacred texts, and so on, of the various world religions. Understanding religious systems, however, gives you limited insight at best into the perspectives and practices of religious believers. Islam is, after all, not the same thing as Muslims. The best way to apprehend religious communities instead of religious systems is to pay close attention to how various groups of believers orient around the central symbols of their religious traditions, to study what the creed "There is no god but God" means in the life and practice of a Muslim, or how the Cross guides believing, behaving, and belonging for Christians. This relationship between believer and tradition is what Cantwell Smith called faith. It was, for him, the most important way to understand how religion is actually lived, and one that religious studies scholars had too often ignored.

A few years after Cantwell Smith published *The Faith of Other Men,* Congress passed the Immigration Act of 1965, legislation that opened America's borders to people from Asia, Africa, and South America, new citizens who brought not

just their professional talents and dreams of economic success but their religious practices as well. The mosques of Lahore started to spring up in Louisville; the Buddhist prayers
of Colombo were now chanted in Cambridge. What was once
an over-there issue for scholars, missionaries and travelers
was now an over-here issue for everyday citizens: Can Hindu
teenagers eat the food served in the hot lunch served at high
schools in Rochester? Will Buddhist women refuse to be ex-
amined by male doctors at hospitals in Denver? When anger
rises in Kashmir, a territory subject to a violent religious and
national dispute between majority-Hindu India and majority-Muslim Pakistan, will anger rise between Indian Hindus
and Pakistani Muslims in Chicago? And when an Evangelical Christian goes to college and meets a Bangladeshi Muslim, each serious about their own faith, which turns will the
conversation take? These are not ultimately questions about
religious systems, they are questions about religious communities. More specifically, they are questions about how
people of different religious communities will interact with
each other. They are interfaith questions. *Inter*—how we relate to the diversity around us. *Faith*—how we orient around
the key symbols of our religious traditions. *Interfaith*—how
our orientation around our religious traditions impacts the
relationship we have with the diversity around us, and how
our relationships with the diversity around us shape the way
we orient around our religious traditions.

One day, as we were preparing for class, Cassie noted
that not only had Cantwell Smith predicted her situation
with Ahmed, he had also pinpointed the particular struggle
she had experienced—namely, how to be a faithful Christian while being friends with a righteous Muslim. "I wish I
had a pastor at the time who understood what I was going
through," she said. It sounded like the perfect assignment
for our class on youth ministry at the Princeton Theological
Seminary.

After Cassie told her story, we split the students up into
pairs and asked one to play the role of the campus pastor and
one to play the role of Cassie, the Christian student who has

recently become friends with a Muslim and is asking a set of questions about her faith, in light of this friendship. As we went around listening in to the conversations, I was struck by how easily the seminary students slipped into the Cassie role. They asked pointed, specific questions:

"Are his beliefs wrong, or are my beliefs wrong?"

"If Islam is evil, like my preacher back home said, how come Ahmed is so nice?"

"I'm friends with this guy—genuinely friends with him. *And* I want to convert him—really, I do. But it feels manipulative to continue a friendship if the only intention I have is to convert someone; it's like a bait and switch. On the other hand, if I continue to be friends with him without telling him about Jesus, I feel like I'm failing my faith."

"Those are precisely the questions I was asking myself at that time," Cassie told me later. The reason, Cassie believed, that they could formulate the questions so clearly was because every student had gone through the experience of being friends with someone from a different faith and through the process asking questions of their own.

The students playing the role of pastor were a different story. Their pastoral skills were impeccable. They listened with soft eyes and offered frequent sympathetic nods. They held the hand of the Cassie character when she grew emotional. But when the faith question was asked, the answer was saccharine. "This is all part of your journey," one said. "Faith and friendship is a mystery," another counseled. Just like the seminary students who had discussed the Grand Island and Jersey City case studies, these students seemed to shy away from Christian language even when presented with a Christian student seeking clarity and confidence from her faith.

Over lunch, the founding director of the seminary's Institute for Youth Ministry, Professor Kenda Dean, shook her head and said, "The church has simply not taught our future leaders a way to articulate Christian identity in a religiously diverse world. We need a language that maintains our own distinctiveness and truth claims while respecting the goodness in others and, above all, affirming the holiness of relationships. The most prevalent Christian language in the public square is the language of domination. Because that language is so ugly and destructive, we race away from it, but we run so far we find ourselves in a land devoid of Christian symbolism entirely."

This was one of the reasons, she believed, for what scholars of the church are calling the trend toward moralistic therapeutic deism, the notion that God exists and is generally good and wants people to be good, but that particular symbols or prayers or practices don't really matter. Carrying the cross gets cumbersome when your friends are Hindus, Muslims, Jews, and humanists. It's easier just to be nice than to talk about being Christian. The phrase "moralistic therapeutic deism," coined by sociologist of religion Christian Smith in a book called *Soul Searching*,[3] was the best way to describe how the majority of young Christians viewed their faith. It was an insight that sent shockwaves through church circles. Christian leaders used to spending a lot of time worrying about the faith of "the unchurched" were stunned to learn that the kids who showed up every week in the pews—"the churched"—didn't know much more than those who didn't come at all. Dean was at the vanguard of addressing the problem, and she was convinced that youth ministry could play a major part. Youth ministry is about engaging young people where they are, swirling about in the carnival of contemporary American cultural diversity, with the fullness of the Gospel. Otherwise, Dean, never one to mince words, believed that youth ministry, like the churches it reflects, would be guilty of promoting the hopelessly benign and acculturated religious outlook suggested by the title of her recent book, *Almost Christian*.[4]

"So, what's wrong with that?" asked Aaron, my friend from graduate school who served as chair of the board of Interfaith Youth Core in the very early days of the organization. He's a nominal Catholic with a big humanist heart, aware of how faith has inspired service but not willing to overlook the violence that religion caused. To him, moralistic therapeutic deism sounds pretty good. It felt like religion minus the dogma.

"It's religion minus the religion," I told him. He looked skeptical. "Listen, maybe this will convince you."

"There is a story of an American Christian pastor who was serving a church in Europe during World War II," I said. "His congregation sent him money so that he could come back and celebrate Christmas with his home church. He used the money to help a group of Jews who would have otherwise burned in Hitler's hellfires flee to safety. One of his congregants got angry when she heard about this and fired off a letter, basically saying, 'How dare you use that money for a different purpose. And those people you helped, they weren't even Christian.' The pastor sent a letter back with these words: 'Yes, but I am.'"

"Faith causes people to do that?" Aaron asked.

"Faith causes people to do that," I said.

"So, how are we going to solve the problem of moralistic therapeutic deism?" he asked.

"Working on it," I told him.

The heart of the matter is how to articulate religious identity in a world of diversity in a way that affirms particularity and builds pluralism. Here is another way of saying that: How can Cassie be a righteous Christian while remaining friends with a good Muslim? Too often, people in that dynamic understand their situation this way: "I'm friends with a Muslim even though I'm Christian." That's not a formulation that says much about either faith or friendship. I think the place we want to get to is this: "*Because* I am a Christian, I have formed a friendship with a Muslim." In other words,

"It is precisely the values that I derive from Christianity that attract me to a person as righteous as you." Here, faith and friendship are connected, mutually enriching instead of mutually exclusive.

When looked at across a religious tradition and a religious population, we recognize that this is a problem whose solution begins with theology and continues into faith formation. Just as the abolition and civil rights movements caused faith communities to articulate a theology of race relations, just as globalization spurred faith communities to articulate a theology of the world church or the global *ummah,* just as climate change has catalyzed articulation of theologies of environmentalism and creation care, the dynamic of increased interaction between people of different faith backgrounds should encourage religious communities to articulate theologies of interfaith cooperation. And just as all of these things were first articulated in books and then worked their way into Sunday school, so must it be with the theology of interfaith cooperation. The most important institution on that road is the seminary, the space within a religious tradition where future religious leaders grapple with questions at the intersection of faith and culture, of history and theology, all with the hope of applying the solutions in the world.

By *theology,* I mean a coherent narrative that references key Scripture, stories, history, heroes, poetry, and so on, from the cumulative historical tradition of the faith community. By *articulate,* I mean to highlight that all our faith traditions already contain resources that speak to positive relations with the religious other. Our challenge is to make those pieces salient, interpret and apply them to the contemporary dynamic of religious diversity, and string them together in a coherent narrative. It is this interpretive process that keeps traditions founded thousands of years ago relevant to the contemporary age. It is what Harvard scholar Diana Eck means when she says that "our religions are more like rivers than monuments, changing."[5]

The seeds of this theology are not in the esoteric or ethereal dimensions of our religions; they are right there at the center, located in what Wilfred Cantwell Smith might call our key symbols. We need to give those key symbols a fresh look, seeing them from the angle of a world defined by interfaith interaction.

In the ten years I have been teaching in seminaries, the Bible story that I have heard most often is the story of the Good Samaritan. It is a story familiar to nearly every Christian, and most non-Christians as well. A lawyer asks Jesus the question "Teacher, how shall I gain eternal life?" Jesus suggests the man answer his own question, based on his knowledge of the holy law: "You shall love the Lord your God with all your heart, with all your soul, with all your strength, and with all your mind—and your neighbor as yourself,"[6] the lawyer dutifully replies.

But then—"desiring to justify himself," the Scripture says—the lawyer presents Jesus with a more complex matter: "Who is my neighbor?" In response, Jesus tells a story:

> A man traveling the road from Jerusalem to Jericho is set on by robbers and left for dead. A priest walks the road, sees the man, and passes to the other side, willfully ignoring him. A Levite does the same. Along comes a traveler, a certain Samaritan, who Jesus says is moved by compassion. He approaches the man, dresses his wounds with oil and wine, places him on his animal, brings him to an inn, and spends the evening caring for him. The next morning, he gives the innkeeper two coins and clear instructions that this man is to be nursed back to full health and that he will pay the additional cost, whatever it may be.
>
> "Now, which of these three do you think seemed to be a neighbor to him who fell among the robbers?" Jesus asks the lawyer.
>
> "He who showed mercy on him," the lawyer responds.
>
> "Go and do likewise," says Jesus.

I imagine Jesus telling this parable about a man from the other community, the despised community, to a large gathering of his main audience—Jews. As Jesus proceeds, describing the brutal robbery, the two men who see and ignore the traveler, and finally the Samaritan who nurses him back to health, I imagine the series of realizations, the layers of understanding, occurring in the minds of this audience.

Clearly, helping those in need is an important part of this story. Well, why don't the priest and the Levite—both representing important positions in the community of Jews—stop to help? They were both aware of the law. In fact, they were expert in the law, and had responsibility for interpreting and implementing it. Perhaps it was their very expertise that prevented them from helping. One of the laws forbade the touching of the dead; another forbade them from touching Gentiles. Perhaps the priest and the Levite feared that the man was dead, or thought he was a Gentile, and chose to follow the letter of the law so that they would not become unclean. Clearly, Jesus is saying there is a good higher than following the letter of the law—the ethic of helping one in need.

But if that were indeed the main point of the story, why not have the priest or the Levite choose to override the letter of the law in the spirit of the higher good? Certainly, that would have brought home the holiness of helping. Something else is happening here.

The priest and the Levite get only three short sentences in the story. The Scripture is not about them. The man who is hurt is also barely described at all. It is the Samaritan who gets all the attention. His actions are described in rich detail—using oil and wine (valuable resources) to dress the wounds, using his own animal to transport the man, spending his own time caring for him, offering the innkeeper whatever money is necessary to nurse him back to health.

Jesus is telling a story about people who were not part of his audience. In fact, he is making one the hero of his story. The Samaritans who were not just "other," and not just despised; they were heretics, *people of a different faith.*

say that the event of this first revelation so frightened the Prophet that he considered flinging himself off the mountain, disgusted that he had allowed himself to become possessed. Khadija calmed her husband, assuring him that Allah would not let a demon enter a servant as righteous as he. She had a cousin, a man named Waraqa, a man learned in the Scriptures, and she would go to him and ask his counsel as to what they should make of these events.

When Waraqa heard the story he exclaimed, "Holy! Holy! . . . There has come to him the great *namus* that came to Moses aforetime, and lo, he is the prophet of his people." When Waraqa next saw Muhammad in Mecca, he ran to kiss the Prophet on the forehead.

Who was Waraqa, I wondered? What did it mean to be "learned in the Scriptures"? It turns out that the first person to recognize the Qur'annic revelation was a Christian, an Arab Christian who never converted to Islam.

The revelations continued, and Muhammad started preaching the message of Islam—mercy and monotheism—in Mecca. As the number of converts grew, so did the anger of the powerful Quraysh tribe. They viewed Muhammad's mission as an insult to their faith and as a threat to their way of life. Attacks on Muhammad and the early Muslims became more brazen, and his companions became afraid for the Prophet's life.

For the Quraysh to rid themselves of Muhammad entirely, they would have to ask the clan leader Abu Talib to lift his protection of the Prophet. The anti-Muhammad forces did not want to risk an internecine war by attacking a man who had the protection of a respected clan leader. Abu Talib was Muhammad's uncle; he had taken Muhammad in after he was orphaned at five years of age. He was also a man fully committed to the pagan gods of Arabia. Muhammad had asked him to convert many times, but Abu Talib had refused. This was one of the points the Quraysh leaders made to him: they collectively belonged to a tradition that Muhammad was effectively saying was wrong. But Abu Talib

When Jesus finishes, he turns to the man who asked, "Who is my neighbor?" and gently suggests he answer the question based on the story he just heard. The lawyer is unable to bring himself to speak of the man the way Jesus does, to say the word *Samaritan*. But he gets the point of the story: "He who showed mercy on him," he tells the teacher. Jesus doesn't force him further. He trusts the moral will work its way through the man's prejudices. The story ends with Jesus telling the lawyer, and the crowd that has gathered, "Go and do likewise."

I imagine the question lingering, the stillness in the air, the sense of joy and fear and desire that this story has provoked in the audience. I imagine them nervously looking around at one another. No heretics here. No despised ones around. No "others" present. The Samaritans are safely elsewhere. I imagine the comfort this community felt being amid their own as the story opened. And then slowly, as the story develops, as the characters are introduced and the action unfolds, a nagging feeling starts to set in. The respected leaders among them—the priest and the Levite—are not the heroes of this story. Elsewhere in the Bible, Jesus makes it clear that he disagrees with the theology of the Samaritans.[7] Still, it is the Samaritan, the heretic, Jesus tells them to emulate. Jesus seems to be saying it is not enough to stay within the fold of the faithful, not enough even to follow the way, the truth, and the life. To attain the eternal, the story suggests, you have to engage with people who believe differently than you.

"How many times did you hear the Good Samaritan story when you were growing up?" I asked my friend April.

"About a thousand," she said.

I wrote about April in my book *Acts of Faith*—she was the first person hired at Interfaith Youth Core with our initial grant of $35,000. Since then she has helped build IFYC into a $4 million organization, running just about every one of our programs along the way, and launching half of them.

She was raised a devout Evangelical Christian in rural Minnesota by a family who believe that faith is about action. Her mother, out of Christian conviction, adopted children. April led not only Bible studies at church but also service and mission trips abroad throughout her high school years. "Jesus taught that you helped people, especially people different from you," she told me. "That's what the Good Samaritan story is all about."

The turning point in April's faith life came when she was president of the Christian Students Group at Carleton College. A mosque in nearby Minneapolis suffered an arson attack, and April received an e-mail requesting that the religious leaders in the area support the Muslim community in its time of need. April immediately shot back a yes. When she brought the idea to the next meeting of the Carleton Christian group, some members had different instincts. A few suggested that this was a good time to proselytize to the Muslims whose prayer space had been destroyed. When April said she had already sent back an e-mail saying she would help, and thought that turning service into evangelism was disingenuous, one person spoke up with indignity, saying, "Those people aren't Christian. They do not believe in Jesus Christ. They pray to a false God. If you help them, you are supporting devil worship." The problem is, those people had not just their instincts, they also had a very clear interpretation of Christian texts. Out came the fangs and the Scripture, and April found herself subject to a session of religious bigotry decorated with Biblical proof texts.

"While you were being barraged with all these verses claiming you should hate people from other religions, why didn't you just tell the story of the Good Samaritan?" I asked.

"I don't know," she said. "I just stayed silent. I let them out-Scripture me, even though I knew the Bible as well or better than any of them. I guess I just never thought about how those stories applied to people from different religions."

And then she turned the tables on me. "If you were in Morocco or Pakistan, and a group of fanatical Muslims burned down a church, how would you convince the local commu-nity that it was part of being Muslim to help the Christian rebuild?" She wanted to know if there was a theology of interfaith cooperation within Islam. I would be lying if I said I had the answer at the tip of my tongue.

One of the hidden dimensions of interfaith cooperation is how it strengthens your own tradition, precisely because when other people ask searching questions like the one April posed to me, you go back in the sources of your faith to find the answer. And who knew that at the source of Islam, contained in the Prophethood and practice of a respected merchant in Mecca named Muhammad, lay a theology of interfaith cooperation?

Every year during the month of Ramadan, Muhammad would make a spiritual pilgrimage to a cave near Mt. Hira, outside of the city of Mecca. On one of the odd nights of the last ten days of that month in 610, while Muhammad was praying on the mountain, he felt a powerful force enveloping his whole body and heard a voice say "*Iqra*," Arabic for *read* or *recite*. At first, Muhammad was terrified. Trembling, he said to the force, "I am not a reciter," meaning that he was not one of the poets of the Arabian desert, figures whose verse was said to be inspired by demonlike creatures called jinns. Again the force enveloped him, again came the command to recite, and again Muhammad said, "I am not a reciter." It happened a third time—the grip, the command, the shock of fear—but during this cycle, Muhammad felt the following words come forth:

"Recite in the name of thy Lord who created!
He createth man from a clot of blood.
Recite: and thy Lord is the Most Bountiful
He who hath taught by the pen,
taught man what he knew not."[8]

It was the first verse of the Qur'an pouring from his lips. Muhammad returned to his wife, Khadija, crawling on his hands and knees, shaking with fear. There are traditions that rebuffed them and refused to lift his protection. "Go and say what you please," he told his nephew, "for by God I will never give you up on any account."

And so it was that the first person to recognize the Prophethood of Muhammad was a Christian and the primary protector of Muhammad during those brutal early years in Mecca was a pagan. Interfaith cooperation was written into the very founding of my faith tradition, and an ethic that continued throughout Muhammad's life. There is a story of the Prophet hosting a Christian delegation in Medina. The Muslims and Christians had a heated debate on the differences between their respective traditions. At one point, the Christians asked for the Prophet's protection so they could leave the city and perform their prayers. The Prophet surprised them by inviting them into his mosque to pray, saying that just because their traditions had differences did not mean that they should not respect and show hospitality to the others' practices.[9]

This story of the Prophet highlights an important distinction—namely, a theology of interfaith cooperation is not about religions being the same, or even an agreement that everyone is going to heaven. A theology of interfaith cooperation does not state that we should not argue about deep cosmic differences. After all, in the story above, the Muslim hosts led by the Prophet were arguing with the Christian delegation about the different Muslim and Christian views of Jesus. Theirs was not a facile exchange along the lines of "You wash your hands before you pray, and I wash mine—we're all the same." Instead, the story shows that, in the midst of an argument about important theological differences, the Muslims and Christians showed each other kindness, respect, and hospitality. It was a theology of interfaith cooperation that focused on building bridges between people of different faiths, not about which religious bridge leads to heaven.

If the Good Samaritan is the most common Christian story cited by my seminary students, Martin Luther King Jr. is the

most quoted Christian hero. My students like to point out to
me that King's commitment to nonviolence was deeply influenced by the work of Mahatma Gandhi. It is one of the most
inspiring examples of religious influence in modern history.
Gandhi's idea of *satyagraha*—literally "love force"—provided
King a new instrument for combating social problems. King
had long believed in Jesus' exhortations to "Turn the other
cheek" and "Love your enemies," but he understood them
as applying to individual relationships. Gandhi's successful campaign of active pacifism against British rule in India convinced King that nonviolence could be employed as
a method of broad social reform. It was an ethic that King
had the opportunity to put into practice in 1955, during the
Montgomery bus boycott, when King was just twenty-six
years old. "Christ furnished the inspiration," King wrote,
"and Gandhi gave us the method."[10]

It is commonplace to trace King's journey down the path
of Gandhian nonviolence, but King followed Gandhi down
another path as well, one that my seminary students are
surprised to hear about: the path of interfaith cooperation.
Gandhi, of course, was not a Christian. And although he
had great respect for the Christian Scriptures, the book that
Gandhi drew his deepest inspiration from was not the Bible,
it was the Bhagavad Gita.

In 1959, King traveled to India to learn more about
Gandhi's life and work, and was struck that Gandhi's movement involved people of all religious backgrounds and that
the Mahatma had ranked interfaith cooperation as one of
his chief goals. Two months after his return from India,
in his Palm Sunday sermon at Montgomery's Ebenezer Baptist Church, King referred to Gandhi as one of the "other
sheep" of Jesus and said, *"It is one of the strange ironies of the
modern world that the greatest Christian of the twentieth century
was not a member of the Christian church."* He ended his sermon
with the following prayer: "O God, our gracious Heavenly
Father, we thank Thee for the fact that you have inspired men
and women in all nations and in all cultures. We call you dif-

ferent names: some call Thee Allah; some call you Elohim; some call you Jehovah; some call you Brahma; and some call you the unmoved Mover."[11]

King's interfaith path involved far more than the study of different religious systems. The man with the bushy beard marching next to King in the famous picture from Selma is Rabbi Abraham Joshua Heschel, a descendant of Eastern European Hasidic rabbis who had escaped the trains running from Warsaw to Auschwitz by six weeks. Instead of secluding himself into a religious bubble in America, Heschel threw himself into the work of the civil rights movement. About walking with King in Selma, Heschel wrote, "Our march was worship. I felt like my legs were praying."[12]

As King connected the civil rights movement to struggles around the world, from hunger in India to war in Vietnam, no contemporary figure influenced him more than the Buddhist monk Thich Nhat Hanh. In his letter nominating Nhat Hanh for the Nobel Peace Prize, King wrote, "He is a holy man. . . . His ideas for peace, if applied, would build a monument to ecumenism, to a world brotherhood, to humanity." In his first major sermon against the Vietnam War, King connected the Christian ethic that brought him to his antiwar conviction with the core lesson he had learned from the faith of other men: "The Hindu-Muslim-Christian-Jewish-Buddhist belief about ultimate reality . . . is that the force of love is the supreme unifying principle of life."[13]

What surprises my seminary students most of all is the place where King began to take Gandhi's work seriously, the site where a theology of interfaith cooperation that shaped the second half of the twentieth century first began: in seminary. As a student at the Crozer Theological Seminary, King came under the spell of Professor George Davis, the son of a union activist, a committed pacifist, and a deep admirer of Gandhi. King took a third of his Crozer courses with Davis, and it was Davis's copy of Frederick Bonn Fisher's *That Strange Little Brown Man of India, Gandhi* that King borrowed and pored over in the library. The message was reinforced by a lecture that King attended in the spring of 1950 at Philadelphia's Fellowship House, where the president of Howard University, Mordecai Johnson, spoke on Gandhi as an embodiment of Christian love. It moved King to buy a stack of books on the Mahatma and his movement.[14] I imagine King marveling at what Gandhi accomplished in the Great Salt March, his mind swirling with Bible verses and Walter Raushenbush quotes, wondering what it meant to admire the inspiration that Gandhi got from Hinduism while staying committed to his own Christian tradition. It occurs to me that the conversations that King must have had at Crozer sixty-five years ago about faith having both roots and wings is very similar to the ones that seminary students are having today.

One of my favorite lines from King is about the origins of his faith commitment: "I am many things to many people, but in the quiet recesses of my heart, I am fundamentally a clergyman, a Baptist preacher. That is my being and my heritage, for I am also the son of a Baptist preacher, the grandson of a Baptist preacher, and the great-grandson of a Baptist preacher." I thought about those lines when I visited the home where King grew up, in Atlanta's Sweet Auburn district. For all that King learned about faith and leadership at Morehouse College and at Crozer, it's that home where the first and most important formation took place. It is the home where the pressures and wonders of religious diversity are first felt, and these days, felt more intensely than ever before. As the founder of an interfaith organization, I thought I knew something about this. And then I had children—and that, as they say, changes everything.

# AMERICAN MUSLIM CHILD

The late writer David Foster Wallace opened his 2005 commencement address at Kenyon College with the story of two young fish on a morning swim. They pass by an older fish, who stops and says, "Morning, boys. How's the water?" The young fish swim on for a bit, and after a while one turns to the other and says, "What the hell is water?"[1]

Wallace uses the story as a meditation on the importance of awareness, but I can't help see it as a metaphor for the consequences of being immersed in a monoculture. The problem with knowing only a single culture or ecology is not only that you don't know others, it's also that you don't really know your own. Not, at least, in the way we moderns understand what it means to know something. Those fish were perfectly comfortable in the water—they could swim, they could breathe, they could eat. But when they were asked to explain, they couldn't do it. They lacked the language, even for a fellow fish, even for themselves. And when the young fish realized this, they couldn't help but be angry.

Imagine these young fish swimming back to the older fish that posed the question and saying, "Since you know so much, Jack, tell us about this thing called water." The older fish begins with the chemical equation—water is $H_2O$. No traction with that. He tries describing the key properties of water. "It's, well, wet," he tells them. No response. They've never known anything but wet. So he begins to explain by way of comparison. He tells tales of the sky and the land, the fabulous creatures that fill both. He speaks of legs for running, wings for flying, points out the fins the young fish have and says that is their version of legs and wings.

He continues, but the young fish are elsewhere now, in their own heads. They have gone from "What the hell is water?" to "What does running feel like? Or flying?" and then to "Why was I cursed with fins instead of blessed with wings?" and "What the hell will I do if I ever meet one of *them?*" Finally, one turns to the other and says, "Have those other places, those other creatures, always existed? Why did it take the old fish so long to tell us about them? *What were the old fish scared of?*"

The more I thought about this story, the more I connected it to the challenges and wonders of being a parent trying to raise religious children in a religiously diverse world.

One afternoon, when my son Zayd was three and my wife had come home early from work to be with him, she called to deliver some news: Zayd was racing his toy cars up and down the hallway of our third-floor condo and chanting, loudly and repeatedly—and in Spanish—the Lord's Prayer.

"Must be Luz," I said.

Luz is our nanny. She is from Colombia, where she had been a judge, and she brought both her high regard for education and her deep Catholic roots with her when she immigrated. She had helped Zayd learn how to write the alphabet and count to a hundred, taught him how to kick a soccer ball, and gotten him out of diapers at a remarkably early age. The love she had for our children was more like that of a grandmother than that of a nanny. I had come home from work more than once and seen them dancing vigorously in the living room to the Red Hot Chili Peppers (Zayd's favorite band). I just shook my head and smiled, thinking, "After eleven hours of playing soccer, chasing him around the park, taking him to the library, making his lunch and his many, many snacks, you have the energy to dance with him? That's love."

When Jesus finishes, he turns to the man who asked, "Who is my neighbor?" and gently suggests he answer the question based on the story he just heard. The lawyer is unable to bring himself to speak of the man the way Jesus does, to say the word *Samaritan*. But he gets the point of the story: "He who showed mercy on him," he tells the teacher. Jesus doesn't force him further. He trusts the moral will work its way through the man's prejudices. The story ends with Jesus telling the lawyer, and the crowd that has gathered, "Go and do likewise."

I imagine the question lingering, the stillness in the air, the sense of joy and fear and desire that this story has provoked in the audience. I imagine them nervously looking around at one another. No heretics here. No despised ones around. No "others" present. The Samaritans are safely elsewhere. I imagine the comfort this community felt being amid their own as the story opened. And then slowly, as the story develops, as the characters are introduced and the action unfolds, a nagging feeling starts to set in. The respected leaders among them—the priest and the Levite—are not the heroes of this story. Elsewhere in the Bible, Jesus makes it clear that he disagrees with the theology of the Samaritans.[7] Still, it is the Samaritan, the heretic, Jesus tells them to emulate. Jesus seems to be saying it is not enough to stay within the fold of the faithful, not enough even to follow the way, the truth, and the life. To attain the eternal, the story suggests, you have to engage with people who believe differently than you.

"How many times did you hear the Good Samaritan story when you were growing up?" I asked my friend April.

"About a thousand," she said.

I wrote about April in my book *Acts of Faith*—she was the first person hired at Interfaith Youth Core with our initial grant of $35,000. Since then she has helped build IFYC into a $4 million organization, running just about every one of our programs along the way, and launching half of them.

She was raised a devout Evangelical Christian in rural Minnesota by a family who believe that faith is about action. Her mother, out of Christian conviction, adopted children. April led not only Bible studies at church but also service and mission trips abroad throughout her high school years. "Jesus taught that you helped people, especially people different from you," she told me. "That's what the Good Samaritan story is all about."

The turning point in April's faith life came when she was president of the Christian Students Group at Carleton College. A mosque in nearby Minneapolis suffered an arson attack, and April received an e-mail requesting that the religious leaders in the area support the Muslim community in its time of need. April immediately shot back a yes. When she brought the idea to the next meeting of the Carleton Christian group, some members had different instincts. A few suggested that this was a good time to proselytize to the Muslims whose prayer space had been destroyed. When April said she had already sent back an e-mail saying she would help, and thought that turning service into evangelism was disingenuous, one person spoke up with indignity, saying, "Those people aren't Christian. They do not believe in Jesus Christ. They pray to a false God. If you help them, you are supporting devil worship." The problem is, those people had not just their instincts, they also had a very clear interpretation of Christian texts. Out came the fangs and the Scripture, and April found herself subject to a session of religious bigotry decorated with Biblical proof texts.

"While you were being barraged with all these verses claiming you should hate people from other religions, why didn't you just tell the story of the Good Samaritan?" I asked.

"I don't know," she said. "I just stayed silent. I let them out-Scripture me, even though I knew the Bible as well or better than any of them. I guess I just never thought about how those stories applied to people from different religions."

And then she turned the tables on me. "If you were in Morocco or Pakistan, and a group of fanatical Muslims burned down a church, how would you convince the local community that it was part of being Muslim to help the Christians rebuild?" She wanted to know if there was a theology of interfaith cooperation within Islam. I would be lying if I said I had the answer at the tip of my tongue.

One of the hidden dimensions of interfaith cooperation is how it strengthens your own tradition, precisely because when other people ask searching questions like the one April posed to me, you go back in the sources of your faith to find the answer. And who knew that at the source of Islam, contained in the Prophethood and practice of a respected merchant in Mecca named Muhammad, lay a theology of interfaith cooperation?

Every year during the month of Ramadan, Muhammad would make a spiritual pilgrimage to a cave near Mt. Hira, outside of the city of Mecca. On one of the odd nights of the last ten days of that month in 610, while Muhammad was praying on the mountain, he felt a powerful force enveloping his whole body and heard a voice say *"Iqra,"* Arabic for *read* or *recite*. At first, Muhammad was terrified. Trembling, he said to the force, "I am not a reciter," meaning that he was not one of the poets of the Arabian desert, figures whose verse was said to be inspired by demonlike creatures called jinns. Again the force enveloped him, again came the command to recite, and again Muhammad said, "I am not a reciter." It happened a third time—the grip, the command, the shock of fear—but during this cycle, Muhammad felt the following words come forth:

"Recite in the name of thy Lord who created!
He createth man from a clot of blood.
Recite: and thy Lord is the Most Bountiful
He who hath taught by the pen,
taught man what he knew not."[8]

It was the first verse of the Qur'an pouring from his lips. Muhammad returned to his wife, Khadija, crawling on his hands and knees, shaking with fear. There are traditions that say that the event of this first revelation so frightened the Prophet that he considered flinging himself off the mountain, disgusted that he had allowed himself to become possessed. Khadija calmed her husband, assuring him that Allah would not let a demon enter a servant as righteous as he. She had a cousin, a man named Waraqa, a man learned in the Scriptures, and she would go to him and ask his counsel as to what they should make of these events.

When Waraqa heard the story he exclaimed, "Holy! Holy! . . . There has come to him the great *namus* that came to Moses aforetime, and lo, he is the prophet of his people." When Waraqa next saw Muhammad in Mecca, he ran to kiss the Prophet on the forehead.

Who was Waraqa, I wondered? What did it mean to be "learned in the Scriptures"? It turns out that the first person to recognize the Qur'annic revelation was a Christian, an Arab Christian who never converted to Islam.

The revelations continued, and Muhammad started preaching the message of Islam—mercy and monotheism—in Mecca. As the number of converts grew, so did the anger of the powerful Quraysh tribe. They viewed Muhammad's mission as an insult to their faith and as a threat to their way of life. Attacks on Muhammad and the early Muslims became more brazen, and his companions became afraid for the Prophet's life.

For the Quraysh to rid themselves of Muhammad entirely, they would have to ask the clan leader Abu Talib to lift his protection of the Prophet. The anti-Muhammad forces did not want to risk an internecine war by attacking a man who had the protection of a respected clan leader. Abu Talib was Muhammad's uncle; he had taken Muhammad in after he was orphaned at five years of age. He was also a man fully committed to the pagan gods of Arabia. Muhammad had asked him to convert many times, but Abu Talib had refused. This was one of the points the Quraysh leaders made to him: they collectively belonged to a tradition that Muhammad was effectively saying was wrong. But Abu Talib rebuffed them and refused to lift his protection. "Go and say what you please," he told his nephew, "for by God I will never give you up on any account."

And so it was that the first person to recognize the Prophethood of Muhammad was a Christian and the primary protector of Muhammad during those brutal early years in Mecca was a pagan. Interfaith cooperation was written into the very founding of my faith tradition, and an ethic that continued throughout Muhammad's life. There is a story of the Prophet hosting a Christian delegation in Medina. The Muslims and Christians had a heated debate on the differences between their respective traditions. At one point, the Christians asked for the Prophet's protection so they could leave the city and perform their prayers. The Prophet surprised them by inviting them into his mosque to pray, saying that just because their traditions had differences did not mean that they should not respect and show hospitality to the others' practices.[9]

This story of the Prophet highlights an important distinction—namely, a theology of interfaith cooperation is not about religions being the same, or even an agreement that everyone is going to heaven. A theology of interfaith cooperation does not state that we should not argue about deep cosmic differences. After all, in the story above, the Muslim hosts led by the Prophet were arguing with the Christian delegation about the different Muslim and Christian views of Jesus. Theirs was not a facile exchange along the lines of "You wash your hands before you pray, and I wash mine—we're all the same." Instead, the story shows that, in the midst of an argument about important theological differences, the Muslims and Christians showed each other kindness, respect, and hospitality. It was a theology of interfaith cooperation that focused on building bridges between people of different faiths, not about which religious bridge leads to heaven.

If the Good Samaritan is the most common Christian story cited by my seminary students, Martin Luther King Jr. is the

most quoted Christian hero. My students like to point out to
me that King's commitment to nonviolence was deeply influenced by the work of Mahatma Gandhi. It is one of the most
inspiring examples of religious influence in modern history.
Gandhi's idea of *satyagraha*—literally "love force"—provided
King a new instrument for combating social problems. King
had long believed in Jesus' exhortations to "Turn the other
cheek" and "Love your enemies," but he understood them
as applying to individual relationships. Gandhi's successful campaign of active pacifism against British rule in India convinced King that nonviolence could be employed as
a method of broad social reform. It was an ethic that King
had the opportunity to put into practice in 1955, during the
Montgomery bus boycott, when King was just twenty-six
years old. "Christ furnished the inspiration," King wrote,
"and Gandhi gave us the method."[10]

It is commonplace to trace King's journey down the path
of Gandhian nonviolence, but King followed Gandhi down
another path as well, one that my seminary students are
surprised to hear about: the path of interfaith cooperation.
Gandhi, of course, was not a Christian. And although he
had great respect for the Christian Scriptures, the book that
Gandhi drew his deepest inspiration from was not the Bible,
it was the Bhagavad Gita.

In 1959, King traveled to India to learn more about
Gandhi's life and work, and was struck that Gandhi's movement involved people of all religious backgrounds and that
the Mahatma had ranked interfaith cooperation as one of
his chief goals. Two months after his return from India,
in his Palm Sunday sermon at Montgomery's Ebenezer Baptist Church, King referred to Gandhi as one of the "other
sheep" of Jesus and said, *"It is one of the strange ironies of the
modern world that the greatest Christian of the twentieth century
was not a member of the Christian church."* He ended his sermon
with the following prayer: "O God, our gracious Heavenly
Father, we thank Thee for the fact that you have inspired men
and women in all nations and in all cultures. We call you dif-

ferent names: some call Thee Allah; some call you Elohim; some call you Jehovah; some call you Brahma; and some call you the unmoved Mover."[11]

King's interfaith path involved far more than the study of different religious systems. The man with the bushy beard marching next to King in the famous picture from Selma is Rabbi Abraham Joshua Heschel, a descendant of Eastern European Hasidic rabbis who had escaped the trains running from Warsaw to Auschwitz by six weeks. Instead of secluding himself into a religious bubble in America, Heschel threw himself into the work of the civil rights movement. About walking with King in Selma, Heschel wrote, "Our march was worship. I felt like my legs were praying."[12]

As King connected the civil rights movement to struggles around the world, from hunger in India to war in Vietnam, no contemporary figure influenced him more than the Buddhist monk Thich Nhat Hanh. In his letter nominating Nhat Hanh for the Nobel Peace Prize, King wrote, "He is a holy man. . . . His ideas for peace, if applied, would build a monument to ecumenism, to a world brotherhood, to humanity." In his first major sermon against the Vietnam War, King connected the Christian ethic that brought him to his antiwar conviction with the core lesson he had learned from the faith of other men: "The Hindu-Muslim-Christian-Jewish-Buddhist belief about ultimate reality . . . is that the force of love is the supreme unifying principle of life."[13]

What surprises my seminary students most of all is the place where King began to take Gandhi's work seriously, the site where a theology of interfaith cooperation that shaped the second half of the twentieth century first began: in seminary. As a student at the Crozer Theological Seminary, King came under the spell of Professor George Davis, the son of a union activist, a committed pacifist, and a deep admirer of Gandhi. King took a third of his Crozer courses with Davis, and it was Davis's copy of Frederick Bonn Fisher's *That Strange Little Brown Man of India, Gandhi* that King borrowed and pored over in the library. The message was reinforced by a lecture that King attended in the spring of 1950 at Philadelphia's Fellowship House, where the president of Howard University, Mordecai Johnson, spoke on Gandhi as an embodiment of Christian love. It moved King to buy a stack of books on the Mahatma and his movement.[14] I imagine King marveling at what Gandhi accomplished in the Great Salt March, his mind swirling with Bible verses and Walter Raushenbush quotes, wondering what it meant to admire the inspiration that Gandhi got from Hinduism while staying committed to his own Christian tradition. It occurs to me that the conversations that King must have had at Crozer sixty-five years ago about faith having both roots and wings is very similar to the ones that seminary students are having today.

One of my favorite lines from King is about the origins of his faith commitment: "I am many things to many people, but in the quiet recesses of my heart, I am fundamentally a clergyman, a Baptist preacher. That is my being and my heritage, for I am also the son of a Baptist preacher, the grandson of a Baptist preacher, and the great-grandson of a Baptist preacher." I thought about those lines when I visited the home where King grew up, in Atlanta's Sweet Auburn district. For all that King learned about faith and leadership at Morehouse College and at Crozer, it's that home where the first and most important formation took place. It is the home where the pressures and wonders of religious diversity are first felt, and these days, felt more intensely than ever before. As the founder of an interfaith organization, I thought I knew something about this. And then I had children—and that, as they say, changes everything.

# AMERICAN MUSLIM CHILD

The late writer David Foster Wallace opened his 2005 commencement address at Kenyon College with the story of two young fish on a morning swim. They pass by an older fish, who stops and says, "Morning, boys. How's the water?" The young fish swim on for a bit, and after a while one turns to the other and says, "What the hell is water?"[1]

Wallace uses the story as a meditation on the importance of awareness, but I can't help see it as a metaphor for the consequences of being immersed in a monoculture. The problem with knowing only a single culture or ecology is not only that you don't know others, it's also that you don't really know your own. Not, at least, in the way we moderns understand what it means to know something. Those fish were perfectly comfortable in the water—they could swim, they could breathe, they could eat. But when they were asked to explain, they couldn't do it. They lacked the language, even for a fellow fish, even for themselves. And when the young fish realized this, they couldn't help but be angry.

Imagine these young fish swimming back to the older fish that posed the question and saying, "Since you know so much, Jack, tell us about this thing called water." The older fish begins with the chemical equation—water is $H_2O$. No traction with that. He tries describing the key properties of water. "It's, well, wet," he tells them. No response. They've never known anything but wet. So he begins to explain by way of comparison. He tells tales of the sky and the land, the

fabulous creatures that fill both. He speaks of legs for running, wings for flying, points out the fins the young fish have
and says that is their version of legs and wings.

He continues, but the young fish are elsewhere now, in
their own heads. They have gone from "What the hell is
water?" to "What does running feel like? Or flying?" and
then to "Why was I cursed with fins instead of blessed with
wings?" and "What the hell will I do if I ever meet one of
*them?*" Finally, one turns to the other and says, "Have those
other places, those other creatures, always existed? Why did
it take the old fish so long to tell us about them? *What were
the old fish scared of?*"

The more I thought about this story, the more I connected it to the challenges and wonders of being a parent trying to raise religious children in a religiously diverse world.

One afternoon, when my son Zayd was three and my wife
had come home early from work to be with him, she called to
deliver some news: Zayd was racing his toy cars up and down
the hallway of our third-floor condo and chanting, loudly
and repeatedly—and in Spanish—the Lord's Prayer.

"Must be Luz," I said.

Luz is our nanny. She is from Colombia, where she had
been a judge, and she brought both her high regard for education and her deep Catholic roots with her when she immigrated. She had helped Zayd learn how to write the alphabet
and count to a hundred, taught him how to kick a soccer
ball, and gotten him out of diapers at a remarkably early
age. The love she had for our children was more like that of
a grandmother than that of a nanny. I had come home from
work more than once and seen them dancing vigorously in
the living room to the Red Hot Chili Peppers (Zayd's favorite band). I just shook my head and smiled, thinking, "After eleven hours of playing soccer, chasing him around the
park, taking him to the library, making his lunch and his
many, many snacks, you have the energy to dance with him?
That's love."

Luz recognized the importance of teaching kids calm as well as encouraging crazy, which is probably where the lesson on the Lord's Prayer came from. She knew Shehnaz and I are Muslim. We talked about it every Ramadan, when I had to explain why I wasn't eating breakfast. She had seen the Arabic calligraphy around our house, the biographies of the Prophet Muhammad, the copies of the Qur'an. After her brother died, I told Luz the prayer Muslims say when we hear of a death—*"Inna Lilahi wa Inna ilahi Rajiun"* ("We are for God, and we return to Him without doubt"). "Very beautiful," she said, repeating the Arabic slowly in her South American accent and giving me a big, teary hug. Still, she didn't see a problem in teaching Zayd a prayer from her Catholic faith. I had to decide if I did.

One of the most frequent questions I receive when I give speeches on interfaith cooperation is whether young people should know their own faith before they engage in interfaith work. My standard response is to tell the story of how babies are delivered in a typical American hospital. I imagine it as an institution founded by Jewish philanthropists (think of Chicago's Mount Sinai Medical Center or Boston's Beth Israel Deaconess Medical Center), with a Muslim doctor presiding over the delivery, a Hindu anesthesiologist administering the epidural, and a Catholic nurse helping the mother push and shooting warning glances at the hyperventilating father-to-be. My point is this: We are literally born into a condition of interfaith interaction. For most of us, the world of religious homogeneity simply doesn't exist anymore. The challenge, then, is to nurture our children into our faith tradition in the world that is—the world of religious diversity.

The answer felt sufficient to me. In fact, I took some pride in it. But some of the questioners gave me looks that suggested they were unconvinced. As the Muslim leader of an interfaith organization, I wasn't sure why they were skeptical. As the Muslim parent of two boys, I get it. These questioners weren't asking about the abstract social dynamics of raising religious children in the modern world, they were asking about the present and particular challenges of raising *their* religious children.

Luz was far from Zayd's only religious influence from a tradition outside of Islam. Zayd attends a Catholic school that has services every Friday, prayer before every meal, and morning readings on Catholic saints. He listens well and learns quickly. On our annual family holiday to Florida, we drove past a statue store, and Zayd pointed out the window and shouted, "Look, Mommy, it's Mary!" He's got the Easter story down pat: The bad people made Jesus go on a cross. They hurt Jesus with nails, but Jesus was still nice to them. Jesus went to the Father for a day, and then he came back. Jesus always makes good choices.

After I told Zayd that his mother's name—Shehnaz— means "pride of the king," I asked him, "Who's the king, love?" The answer I was hoping for couldn't have been more obvious. Zayd didn't catch the hint. His answer came swift and strong. "The king, daddy, is Jesus."

Should I tell Zayd that Jesus is not the king? Should I expect him to pray in Arabic before meals at school while the other kids are all chanting "In the name of the Father, the Son, and the Holy Ghost"? We tell his teachers not to give him any pork—no pepperoni on pizza day, no ham on Green Eggs and Ham Day. Do we tell them Zayd needs to go somewhere else during the Easter lesson? Do I just let Zayd sit through that and then tell him at home that we don't believe Jesus died on the cross and we don't believe that God has a son, but we do believe that Jesus forgave the many people that were not nice to him, that he always made good choices, and that he is definitely part of God's royalty? As clear as I felt giving sociological answers on the interfaith moment from the stage, I felt confused in nurturing my child's Muslim identity on the multifaith playground.

Not just confused, actually—afraid. Would he say Catholic prayers so many times that they felt more natural to him than Muslim prayers? Would he simply ignore me when I told him the *Muslim* story of Jesus?

Around the time I was worrying about Catholic teaching, we got invited to the birthday party of Zayd's Jewish friend Ariel. It was at a petting zoo, and there was plenty of Zayd's favorite cake, but the thing that stuck with Zayd was all the people saying, *"Mazel tov."*

"Daddy, why do they keep saying that?" he asked. "What does it mean?"

"It means 'Congratulations,'" I told him. "People say that when something good happens to someone. Today is Ariel's birthday, so everyone is congratulating him."

"Why don't they just say 'Congratulations,' then?" he asked me.

"Well, they're Jewish," I said. "When something is a very special occasion, they want to say congratulations in their language."

"Hmmm," Zayd said. "What will you say to me on my birthday?"

I was about to say the obvious—"Happy birthday"—but something made me stop in my tracks. Zayd had heard "Happy birthday" plenty before. That's not the answer he was looking for. And he hadn't asked me to say, *"Mazel tov"* to him. He wanted to know if *we* had something like *"Mazel tov,"* something distinct that *we* said to mark special occasions. He wanted the version of *"Mazel tov"* that was his.

*"Mubaraki,"* I told him. "I will say, '*Mubaraki*' to you on your birthday!" I happily launched into a lecture on the term *mubaraki*—how it is from *our* holy language and it is *our* way of saying, "Very special congratulations." (Actually, *mubaraki* is the South Asian Hindi/Urdu derivation of the Arabic term *mabrook,* but I decided on the shortcut explanation with Zayd.)

This was a novel insight. My son's encounters with other people's religious language and stories actually made his own faith more relevant. Religion was not just something he did for a few moments before bed and meals, or for a few hours a week at religious education lessons, it was something all around him—at school, at Saturday-morning birthday parties. The more he was around other people's religions, the more he wanted to know about his own.

Every time Zayd came home with a Jesus story or a Christian prayer, I sat down and taught him a Muhammad story and a Muslim prayer. Zayd's encounters with other religions gave me a reason to talk with him about his own. I tried to do it in a way that highlighted the shared values across both traditions. In the Christian story of Jesus, he forgives the people who put him on the cross, returning kindness for hate. There is a similar story about the Prophet Muhammad. Every day, he walks under a balcony in Mecca, where a woman throws trash on him. The Prophet never gets angry with the woman or even scolds her. One day, the Prophet realizes that there is no trash coming from the balcony. He looks up and doesn't see the woman. Instead of rejoicing over her absence, or even considering it an act of God that she didn't show up, the Prophet becomes concerned about the woman's health. After being told that she has indeed taken very ill, the Prophet brings her water and prays for her recovery. "Like Jesus, the Prophet Muhammad always makes good choices," I emphasized.

My mind started adapting my graduate school comparative-religions charts for a toddler. They say, "*Mazel tov*"; we say, "*Mubaraki*." They have a name for and a description of God (the Lord, our Father); we have a name for and a description of God (Allah the Creator). They have a Jesus story (the son who died on the cross); we have a Jesus story (the Prophet who brought and embodied God's message of love and forgiveness). They have Catholic saints; we have Shia *imams*. They have hymns; we have Ismaili *ginans*.

There's the category of things every religion shares: thanking God before meals and bedtime is important. There's the category of things we share with Jews: we don't eat pork, we pray in a language other than English. There's the category of things we share with Christians: Jesus always makes good choices. There's the category we share specifically with Christians who are Catholics: incense means something holy is about to happen.

The twentieth-century African American writer James Baldwin tells the story about when he was living in a Swiss village while finishing work on a book.[2] Walking through the town square one afternoon, answering the questions of little Swiss children who were touching his hair, asking him what he eats, if he sleeps at night, he has a sudden realization: he is not simply the only black person in this village, he is also the only black person these people have ever seen. He ends the essay with this observation: the world, once white, is white no more, and will never be white again.

Those villagers were going to have to come to an understanding of who they were in a world where at least one person in their presence was not like them. British scholar Anthony Giddens says it's this dynamic that makes the modern world so challenging to negotiate. When you encounter a person with a pattern of life different than your own—someone who doesn't go to church on Sunday in a town of Christians, someone who doesn't pray in Arabic in a village of Muslims—you start to ask yourself a series of questions that most human beings through most of human history, raised as they were in monocultures, never had to deal with: If they don't go to church on Sunday, why do I? If I have been taught that my way is the best way, what do I think of their way? When I pass them on the street, what do I say?

It is precisely the situation in which the two rabbis in writer Chaim Potok's *Book of Lights* find themselves. On a trip to Japan, while observing the rituals of a Shinto priest, one rabbi looks at the other and says, "Is God listening to this? If not, why not? If so, what are we about?"[3]

For Zayd, for most of us, there is no pre-Baldwin Swiss village—no island, no retreat, no bubble—to protect us from the jazz and war of the world's diversity. The question is, How do parents and religious communities make this an asset in faith formation rather than an obstacle? When do we realize that it is the jazz and war of the world that our faiths are meant for?

———

It's not just Catholics and Jews that Zayd interacts with. Our neighbors next door are secular Hindus, and their five-year-old son, Karthik, is Zayd's best friend. Zayd was uncharacteristically quiet for most of the Diwali party Karthik's parents hosted in 2010. But when the food came, he looked over at his friend and said, "Karthik, you need to say, '*Shukrun lillah*' before you eat."

I was one proud papa witnessing that moment. "He remembers a Muslim prayer," I thought to myself. "And he's willing to say it, even though it's outside of our house and his Muslim religious-education lessons."

My flush of pride was interrupted by Zayd's rising voice. He was insisting, at the top of his lungs, that Karthik say, "*Shukrun lillah.*"

Karthik knew how to play this game. He smiled sweetly, a young child intent on getting under his friend's skin, and shook his head no as if denying Zayd a toy that he wanted to play with.

This, of course, just made Zayd fill his lungs with a new whoosh of air and level the command out at an even higher volume: "YOU HAVE TO SAY '*SHUKRUN LILLAH*' BEFORE YOU EAT!"

I swear that Karthik's parents shot Shehnaz and me a look that said, "We thought you weren't *those* kinds of Muslims." Shehnaz shot me a look that very clearly said, "You're the religion guy—you take care of this. I made the cupcakes."

Zayd was crying now, alternately asking aloud, "Why won't Karthik say '*Shukrun lillah?*'" and whimpering softly, "Karthik, you have to say '*Shukrun lillah.*'" He got up and started toward Karthik, who was still smiling sweetly, keeping his toy away. "Uh-oh—this is not good," I thought to myself. Zayd was going through a hitting phase. His friend at school had recently gotten whacked with a marker on the forehead. "Why'd you hit Jose?" I asked him. "Because he was running faster than me in the race," Zayd told me, his eyes growing dark. That was the look I was seeing now.

I put my food down and took off, intercepting Zayd a few steps from Karthik. I picked him up in my arms and blurted out the first thing that came to my mind: "Karthik doesn't have to say, '*Shukrun lillah*,' love. We say, '*Shukrun lillah*' for Karthik. I want you to go back to your plate and close your eyes and think of your food and Karthik and everything and everybody you love and say, '*Shukrun lillah*'—you're thanking God for all of it. How does that sound?"

Zayd, remarkably, thought it sounded good. He wiped away a tear and nodded his head. I turned to Karthik, who was calmly eating his meal. He nodded, too. It was okay with him if he was included in Zayd's prayers. My wife gave me a "Not bad" look.

It wasn't until later that night—party over, kids in bed, small space to reflect on the day—that I realized I might have stumbled onto something very important. In a world of lots of different people and prayers, of religious narratives that intersect here, diverge there, oppose elsewhere, perhaps the most important and relevant lesson we teach our religious children is this: *your* religion is even more relevant in this cacophonous world because it marks your concern with and care for your friends from *all* religions.

"*Mubaraki*," I said to Zayd on his fourth birthday. "*Mubaraki*," I said again, this time with added fatherly emphasis. He smiled faintly at me, and then went back to eating pizza with his friends. I admit to feeling a little disappointment. The "*Mazel tov*" moment had been such a big insight for me, but maybe for Zayd it amounted to just one more interesting feature of an endlessly interesting world.

Later that afternoon, when we were opening presents, I saw Zayd gravitate toward the ones that looked like they might have remote-controlled cars inside. I snuck a package of what felt like books in front of him. Reluctantly, he opened it. One had an azure cover with the outline of a man riding a smiling horse flying through the night sky: *Muhammad*, by Demi.[4] Shehnaz and I smiled at each other.

"Zayd, look," I said. "It's a book about the Prophet Muhammad." But Zayd was already tearing into the next package, hoping for that remote-controlled car. I opened the book, started turning the pages, and was struck by the beauty of the illustrations transposed with verses from the Qur'an. I figured maybe one of Zayd's grandmothers, or an aunt, had given it to him. I opened the card. It was from Karthik.

"Zayd, Karthik gave this to you," I said.

Zayd turned back. "Karthik gave me that book?" he asked.

"Yep," I said.

He took it and opened the pages. "Karthik knows about the Prophet Muhammad?" Zayd asked.

"He sure does," I said.

All the mealtime prayers and bedtime stories about religion, all the hours spent in religious-education classes with his grandmother—nothing seemed to interest Zayd in his own faith as much as the idea that his friend from a different tradition respected it.

Sometimes you need to know a little about the sky to appreciate the ocean. Sometimes you need a bird to tell you that it's cool to be a fish.

# CONCLUSION

When the news reports started airing of a bomb in central Oslo, Pamela Geller did what Pamela Geller does: she posted pieces on her website blaming Muslims. "Jihad in Norway?" she asked. Then, "You cannot avoid the consequences of ignoring Jihad." As the story about the attacks on the island of Utoya started taking shape, more and more media figures pointed their fingers in the same direction as Geller. Happy for the company but angry at their word choice, she snapped on her blog, "If I hear another television or radio reporter refer to Muhammad as 'the *Prophet* [italics in original] Muhammad,' I think I am going to puke. He's not your prophet, assclowns."[1]

It turns out that all those fingers should have been pointing the other way. The man who rented a farm in rural Norway to practice making bombs, who took a ferry to the island of Utoya, where, dressed in a police officer's uniform, he shot several dozen teenagers at a youth camp, cited as his reason the hatred of Muslims and named as one of his inspirations Pamela Geller's blog. Geller's friend Robert Spencer, author of ten books with titles like *Religion of Peace? Why Christianity Is and Islam Isn't,* was referenced 162 times in perpetrator Anders Breivik's manifesto.[2] In the summer of 2010, the industry of Islamophobia in America had succeeded in drawing a straight line between Muslims who wanted to build an interfaith center near Ground Zero to the Muslims who attacked the World Trade Center. The following summer, they were accused of motivating a mass-murder spree an ocean away.

Rabbi Abraham Joshua Heschel once said, "Speech has power. Words do not fade. What starts out as a sound, ends in a deed."[3] Contemporary analysts seemed to agree. Marc Sageman, a forensic psychiatrist and former CIA officer, pointed out that just as al-Qaeda emerged out of the intellectual infrastructure of extremist Muslim ideology, so Anders Breivik drew from a similar poison in a different well. "This rhetoric," Sageman told the *New York Times*'s Scott Shane, "is not cost-free." Daryl Johnson, a former US Department of Homeland Security official and, during his tenure there, primary author of a report called "Right Wing Extremism," said, "It could easily happen here." The Hutaree, an extremist militia based in Michigan, had more weapons in its arsenal than all the Muslim plotters charged in the United States since 9/11 combined.[4]

I admit to jumping on the bandwagon for a few days, gleefully following the tweets and articles calling Breivik a Christian terrorist. In a piece comparing Breivik to Oklahoma City bomber Timothy McVeigh, former American Academy of Religion president Mark Jurgensmeyer wrote, "Both were good-looking young Caucasians, self-enlisted soldiers in an imagined cosmic war to save Christendom. Both thought their acts of mass destruction would trigger a battle to rescue society from the liberal forces of multiculturalism that allowed non-Christians and non-whites positions of acceptability . . . both were Christian terrorists."[5] Jurgensmeyer pointed out that the date Breivik had chosen for his murder spree, July 22, was the same date that the Kingdom of Jerusalem was established during the First Crusade.

After being subject to a daily barrage about the evils in one's own faith, I suppose it is only natural to happily highlight how another religion can motivate horror. But it's not what interfaith leaders do. It was a lesson I learned at an interfaith conference in Australia.

It was a major event that took place in the Australian

Houses of Parliament, in Canberra. There were major politicians and religious figures on the speakers' list, and an audience full of leading citizens and media figures. Television cameras typically do not show up for interfaith conferences unless they are promised a cage fight, and for this particular session at least, the organizers delivered. The main event was a debate between a fiery Christian figure and an imam. And, no surprise, they'd gotten the scariest-looking Muslim they could find. Imposingly tall, sporting a regulation-size beard, wearing a dark, flowing robe, and carrying a staff, he looked like he'd walked out of a twelfth-century cave. "Oh, God," I thought. "He's the very picture of a medieval Muslim."

The Christian evangelist, wearing a sharp suit and cool eyeglasses, went first. He spoke of the hatred and harassment he experienced growing up in a village in Pakistan: "I was beaten. My church was burned. My family was threatened. Never once did a Muslim stand up for me or offer to protect me."

It sounded terrible. It also sounded rehearsed. This was probably how this guy made his living, going to conferences and telling stories about how the evil Muslims from over there were now flooding here. It seemed that the industry of Islamophobia was everywhere. But this guy was different in how far he was prepared to go. "I am only grateful that they did not follow their religion completely," he added. "If they did, it would have been worse. Then they would have killed me, probably beheaded me. They would have taken my wife and had their way. That is what their terrorist religion would have made them do. It is what the greatest terrorist of all time, their leader and founder, the Prophet Muhammad, would have told them."

I felt my throat getting tight and the hair on the back of my neck start to rise. I started scribbling down examples of Christian violence. You want Scripture? How about "Dash their children against the stones," from Deuteronomy.[6] You want historical examples? How about the Inquisition? Now I was glad the caveman Muslim was representing me. I was glad he was carrying a staff and looked medieval. I wanted him to turn directly to this guy, bare his big, scary, stained teeth, and let loose with a stream of examples of Christian ugliness.

But my guy was not baring his teeth or shaking his staff. He was not trying to be intimidating at all. He was listening calmly. And when he spoke, his voice was soft and gentle:

> I think perhaps you expect me to respond to your insults of my religion with insults to your religion. But I cannot do that, even if I want to. I respect too much your faith. I love too much your founder, the Prophet Jesus. I wish only that you knew the truth about the Prophet Muhammad. How, like Jesus, he revealed God's message of mercy. I am sad that you did not know more Muslims in Pakistan who you could call friends, who protected your family from thugs and brutes. If I were in Pakistan, I would have stood up for you. My commitment to following the Prophet Muhammad requires me to.

There is a story that Sufi Muslims tell of Jesus—that when he was in the market in Jerusalem and people came up to insult him, he turned around and blessed them. When, later, his disciples asked how he could bless people who insulted him, Jesus responded, "I give only what I carry in my purse."

"And we are put on Earth a little space," poet William Blake wrote, "that we may learn to bear the beams of love."[7] Of all the wide knowledge there is to learn in interfaith literacy, of all the intricate skills necessary to be an interfaith organizer, by far the most important quality for an interfaith leader is an orientation toward love.

In the final days of the Montgomery bus boycott, after 380 days of walking to work and suffering arbitrary arrests, phantom death threats, and one very real house bombing, Dr. Martin Luther King Jr. gave a speech in Montgomery where he said, "We have before us the glorious opportunity to inject a new dimension of love into the veins of our civilization. . . . The end is reconciliation, the end is redemption, the end is the creation of the beloved community."[8]

People say that spirit is gone, but I know that's not true. King was a twenty-year-old student when he learned of Gandhi, a twenty-six-year-old recent seminary graduate when he was selected to lead the bus boycott. Part of the joy of working on college and seminary campuses, training a critical mass of students and recent graduates to be interfaith leaders, is seeing the spirit of King and Gandhi resurrected in them.

Sometimes, even the most unlikely ones. Audrey was the quietest intern at Interfaith Youth Core in the summer of 2010. She had grown up in a small town in California and had read about IFYC when she was a student at Chico State University and had come to intern with us the summer after she graduated, not sure what was next for her. When I held my final session with the interns and asked how they planned to apply their interfaith-leadership skills on campus or back home, she was the one intern who said she didn't really know. But when a chain e-mail titled "Can Muslims Be Good Americans" started making the rounds of her church, she knew she had to do something. The e-mail listed ten reasons, including the following:

- Theologically—no . . . Because his allegiance is to Allah, the moon god of Arabia.
- Socially—no . . . Because his allegiance to Islam forbids him to make friends with Christians or Jews.
- Spiritually—no . . . Because when we declare "one nation under God," The Christian's God is loving and kind while Allah is NEVER referred to as Heavenly Father.

"Maybe this is why our American Muslims are so quiet and not speaking out about any atrocities," a church leader had noted at the top of the e-mail.

Audrey and a friend wrote in response, "It saddens us to read such hateful, ignorant, and biased remarks. Our country was founded on freedom of religion. . . . Shouldn't [Christians] be praying and setting an example?" They hit Reply All, thinking that was the end of it.

Nothing could have prepared Audrey for the volley of hatred that followed. For the next several days, her in-box was filled with vitriol from people she had sat in the pews with since she was a little girl:

> "Audrey, Where are you going to University? Mecca U?"

> "Audrey, You are deceived. Have you been to your mosque lately? Got muslim lady costume?"

> "Christians are supposed to be Faith Defenders. You instead are a Moslem lover. There is no such thing as a 'Good Moslem.'"

She had to leave her church, my IFYC colleague Amber told me, the church she had been baptized in. I felt terrible. The last thing I wanted was for interfaith work to separate somebody from their religion.

I called her to ask how she was doing, and also to apologize. I was prepared to talk with her family, anything. These had been the most difficult days of her life, she told me. "My best friends were at that church. The adults that I respected the most in the world were at that church. I was literally texting with them casually until I sent that e-mail, and then they treated me like I was a monster." I apologized again, but she interrupted:

> I made friends with all these people from different faiths at Interfaith Youth Core. I couldn't stand thinking that members of my church were insulting good people they'd never met because of these lies in

a chain e-mail. I mean, every week at Interfaith Youth Core, I went and did a service project with Muslims, Jews, and humanists. It was a great experience. I just didn't know how to take it back to my community or how it related to me being a Christian. Well, these last few days, I've been reading the Bible a lot, and here's what I realized: Sending that e-mail and standing up for Muslims was the most Christian thing I have ever done.

She'd returned to California from her internship at Interfaith Youth Core unsure of her next steps. But they were clear now: She wanted to go to seminary. She wanted to learn more about the religions of the people she'd met at IFYC and more about what her Christian faith says about being in relationship with them. And wherever she wound up, as a pastor or a college chaplain or a professor of comparative religion, she wanted to create experiences where people from different faiths were meeting each other, learning from one another, building interfaith bridges high enough to rise over the barriers and strong enough to withstand the bombs.

One more interfaith leader committed to securing the blessings of pluralism on America's sacred ground.

# AFTERWORD

By Martin E. Marty

Seven Deadly Sins of the college campus—ignorance, intolerance, apathy, unawareness, prejudice, distraction, and exclusiveness—frequently appear in registers of "what's wrong" with the young. Eboo Patel has seen them all, since he and his colleagues have been involved with scores of colleges, universities, and seminaries. I write "Seven Deadly Sins" rather than "*the* Seven Deadly Sins" because Patel and his coworkers could add many more to the list from what they have seen.

Patel can be disappointed, disturbed, and frankly terrified by some of what he has seen and what he knows other citizens have also experienced. Yet were he merely to report or, worse, whine over what he has seen, readers who have better things to do would soon toss his book aside. He does more than report about bad things, aware as he is that he can also find seven times seven virtues on campuses, at community gatherings, and in religious institutions. How to help turn the proverbial "sins" to "virtues" has been his goal, and he has worked impressively to achieve it, as this book attests, without boasting.

If I have made it seem as if educational institutions monopolize the attention of Patel and his readers, this is not the case. Patel has focused on them because they are efficient and decisive locales for encountering and engaging the young. He has sat in on and no doubt walked away from countless gatherings of attentive citizens who listened to lectures, watched PowerPoint presentations, and observed dramatizations designed to promote the common good. What most of these gatherings shared was the age of those present, which in most cases was "middle" through "senior." Where were the young? He has nothing against citizens "post-youth," knowing that if we are fortunate we may all get to that stage, and he is getting toward it himself.

But where were the young in the movements of the recent past? Why were they not there? Why did they turn out for athletics, entertainment, and celebrity appearances but were turned off by or away from the "common good" events? As part of Patel's answer he created Interfaith Youth Core, to help understand the old ways of the young and to assist them in finding new ways. This focus was and is worthwhile, as there are so many who belong to younger generations. Patel's focus on the campus is doubly worthwhile because of the impact of higher education on the larger culture.

As I first read *Sacred Ground,* I kept noticing how seldom Patel used a good word that had once served well: tolerance. I thought that it should have been fitting still. But he knows how often "tolerance" and its synonyms turn out to be bland and ineffective as part of a strategy or a lure. Reading on, I also watched for alternatives to "tolerance," and even searched the text in order to test what was so noticeable: Patel uses "interfaith" more often than "tolerance." This is natural, a reader might say, because the word is in the very title of the organization, program, and commitment of this alternative, as in *Interfaith* Youth Core.

Why does this difference make a difference?" (And, along the way, let me hasten to say: Don't throw away "tolerance" or "toleration." They can come back to serve fresh purposes after our society does some reevaluating of what has gone wrong and what might help make it right.) Here is the theme that Patel has brought to the forefront of his discoveries: "Faith," that grand and profound element in "the faiths," "the religions," and "the believing communities," across the board was being corrupted in our time and used as an instrument of tribalism, exclusivism, xenophobia, hatred, and killing. Check the headlines and observe how often groups have been warring in the name of their God or their gods, denigrating those who are "other" to them.

Then note the too-few movements of dialogue among faith groups and stories of common participation in sacrificial and noble acts, and notice how much IFYC has achieved despite its lack of resources, publicity, or celebrity. I have observed Patel and IFYC in semi-public gatherings as they planned for their public offerings on campuses. The sessions were instructional, showing attention to detail without which a movement such as this stands little chance of surviving or finding itself ready for change as changes come. It impresses those of us who represent informal "Interfaith Aged Cores" to see how democratic and trusting the young participants are.

Odds are that in the next generation, those who look in on agencies and gatherings promoting the interfaith movement will be able to enjoy seeing and learning from participants who are often less gray or bald or slowed down than many are today. (But may older participants continue to make their contributions.) The goals and tactics of IFYC are portable, transformable, and exemplary. Patel has argued for and contributed to such movements, so that they together can achieve much more in the crucial decades ahead. For now, he is busy with IFYC, and we readers can be engrossed in its story, even as we keep the larger culture in mind. Patel tells stories and gives often implicit advice about what Interfaith Youth Core and its kin can set out to achieve. People of all ages, whether on campuses or not, will pick up advice and likely experience a boost in morale and resolve.

—Martin E. Marty
*Fairfax M. Cone Distinguished*
*Service Professor Emeritus*
University of Chicago

# ACKNOWLEDGMENTS

When I mentioned to the Reverend Michael Garanzini, SJ, the president of Chicago's Loyola University, that I was looking for a quiet place to work on a book, I was hoping maybe he'd find me a large broom closet somewhere in the Education Department. Instead, he suggested that I use his personal office overlooking Lake Michigan. His generosity was matched by the graciousness of the staff and administrators in Burrowes Hall who were my colleagues over the course of the summer of 2011, especially Dipti Shah, whose smiles greeted me every morning and whose frowns told me it was time to stop staring out across the lake and focus back on the computer. Thank you also to Tara and the crew at The Grind, who always give me coffee from the most freshly brewed pot, extra-toast my bagels just so, never roll their eyes at such requests, and therefore provide the perfect environment for a writer to work on his craft.

I am eternally grateful to the board of Interfaith Youth Core and, especially, its chair, Howard Morgan, for giving me the time and space away from managing the organization to gather my thoughts and write this book. They are a rare group of directors, individuals who care deeply about the mission and impact of this organization, and equally for the people who staff it. I am proud to work for them.

I am indebted to Barbara McGraw, coeditor of *Taking Religious Pluralism Seriously: Spiritual Politics on America's Sacred*

*Ground,* for our conversations connecting interfaith cooperation and sacred ground in America.

My editor, Amy Caldwell, did for this book what she does
for all books: made it better. I am thankful for her sharp in-
sights. Thank you to my agent, Don Fehr, for giving me the
sage advice that the best publisher for this, my second book,
was the publisher of my first: Beacon Press. Working with
Don was great, and being a part of Beacon—the press that
has published the works of personal heroes of mine from
James Baldwin to Geoffrey Canada—is an honor.

Thank you to Rabbi Or Rose, Professor Charles Cohen,
the Reverend Dr. Kenda Dean, Jenan Mohajir, Peter Gil-
mour, and Tom Levinson for your insightful comments on
the manuscript. Special thanks to Claire Albert, who worked
with me every step of the way on this manuscript, from the
initial ideas to the final endnotes. Thank you to the terrific
staff of IFYC and the network of young interfaith leaders we
have the pleasure to work with. You will recognize much of
this book. The best ideas were formed in discussions with
you. The best stories are inspiring tales of the bridges you
have built. Advancing this movement with you is nothing
short of a thrill.

And to my family—my parents and brother, who have
only been encouraging, my wife, who was blessed with im-
measurable grace, and my children, who constantly amaze
me by going at Mach 5 *all the time*—what can I say except that
I wish I deserved how good you are to me.

# NOTES

## INTRODUCTION

1. Pew Research Center, "Views of Religious Similarities and Differences: Muslims Widely Seen as Facing Discrimination," Pew Forum on Religious and Public Life, 2009 Annual Religion and Public Life Survey, http://pewforum.org/.

2. Quoted in Maria Rosa Menocal, *The Ornament of the World: How Muslims, Jews, and Christians Created a Culture of Tolerance in Medieval Spain* (New York: Little, Brown, 2002).

3. Ibid., 22–23.

4. Michael Walzer, *What It Means to Be an American* (New York: Marsilio, 1996), 55.

5. Barack Obama, "President Barack Obama's Inaugural Address," January 21, 2009, *The White House,* http://www.whitehouse.gov/.

6. Martin Luther King Jr., "Beyond Vietnam: A Time to Break Silence," April 4, 1967, *American Rhetoric,* http://www.americanrhetoric.com/.

7. There is an alternate version of this in which the real estate developer Sharif El-Gamal is at the center of the story and calls the project Park51. For a good description, see Mark Jacobson, "Muhammad Comes to Manhattan," *New York,* August 22, 2010, http://nymag.com/.

8. Ralph Blumenthal and Sharaf Mowjood, "Muslim Prayers and Renewal Near Ground Zero," *New York Times,* December 8, 2009.

9. *The O'Reilly Factor,* Fox News, December 21, 2009.

10. Omid Safi, *Progressive Muslims: On Justice, Gender, and Pluralism* (New York: Oneworld, 2003).

11. Eboo Patel, *Acts of Faith: The Story of an American Muslim, the Struggle for the Soul of a Generation* (Boston: Beacon, 2007).

12. Max DePree, *Leadership Is an Art* (New York: Dell, 1990), 11.

13. Surah al-Hujurat 49:13.

14. Justin Kaplan, ed., *Whitman: Poetry and Prose* (New York: Literary Classics of the United States, 1982), 956.

## GROUND ZERO

1. Kirk Semple, "Council Votes for Two Muslim School Holidays," *New York Times,* June 30, 2009.

2. Ibid.

3. Celeste Katz, "Carl Paladino Advertises on Ground Zero Mosque Issue," *New York Daily News,* August 5, 2010, http://www.nydailynews .com/.

4. Peter Nicholas and Julia Love, "Obama Supports Plan for Mosque Near Ground Zero," *Los Angeles Times,* August 14, 2010, http://www.latimes.com.

5. Michael Barbaro, "Mayor's Stance On Muslim Center Has Deep Roots," *New York Times,* August 12, 2010, http://www.nytimes.com.

6. To its credit, the Anti-Defamation League—after the furor around their anti–Cordoba House position—launched a robust task force providing legal defense for mosques being opposed in various communities across the United States. As this is in line with the high ideals of the ADL, I am proud to be part of this group. For more information, see my "Why I Joined Abe Foxman's Anti-Islamophobia Task Force," *Huffington Post,* September 7, 2010, http://www.huffingtonpost.com/.

7. Barbaro, "Mayor's Stance On Muslim Center Has Deep Roots."

8. For first speech, see Justin Elliott, "Michael Bloomberg Delivers Stirring Defense of Mosque," *Salon,* August 3, 2010, http://salon .com. For second speech, see *Wall Street Journal* Staff, "Bloomberg on Mosque: 'A Test of Our Commitment to American Values," *Wall Street Journal,* August 24, 2010, http://www.wsj.com.

9. Sharon Otterman, "Obscuring a Muslim Name, and an American's Sacrifice," *New York Times,* January 1, 2012, http://newyorktimes .com.

10. Michael Barbaro, "N.Y. Political Leaders' Rift Grows on Islam Center," *New York Times,* August 24, 2010, http://www.nytimes.com.

11. Ibid.

12. Kenneth T. Jackson, "A Colony With a Conscience," *New York Times,* December 27, 2007, http://www.nytimes.com.

13. "Remonstrance of the Inhabitants of the Town of Flushing to Governor Stuyvesant, December 27, 1657," *Flushing Monthly Meeting of the Religious Society of Friends (Quakers),* http://www.nyym.org/ flushing/.

14. George Washington, "To Bigotry No Sanction," American Treasures, Library of Congress, August 17, 1790, http://www.loc.gov/.

15. Steven Waldman, *Founding Faith: Providence, Politics, and the Birth of Religious Freedom in America* (New York: Random House, 2009), 65.

16. Paul F. Boller, *George Washington and Religion* (Dallas: Southern Methodist University, 1963), 120.

17. Langston Hughes, "Let America Be America Again," 1935, from *The Collected Poems of Langston Hughes* (New York: Knopf, 1994).

18. Rev. Dr. Martin Luther King Jr., "The American Dream," February 5, 1964, from "Online Exhibits," Drew University Online Archives, http://depts.drew.edu/.

19. Walt Whitman, *Whitman: Poetry and Prose* (New York: Literary Classics of the United States, 1982), 50.

20. Eboo Patel, "On Muslims, Gays and Tolerance in America," *Huffington Post,* December 28, 2010, http://www.huffingtonpost.com.

21. Nico Lang, "Dreaming of a 'Different World,'" *Faith Divide* blog, *Washington Post,* February 15, 2011, onfaith.washingtonpost.com.

22. Jalaludin Rumi, from "Masnavi-I Ma'navi," in *Teachings of Rumi,* trans. by Idries Shah (London: Octagon Press, 1994).

23. Umar Faruq Abdullah, "Islam and the Cultural Imperative" (Chicago: Nawawi Foundation, 2004).

24. In early 2012, Mayor Bloomberg was again in the news on issues related to Muslims. This time, in my opinion, he was on the wrong side. Bloomberg was a strong supporter of the New York Police Department's surveillance of Muslims, for the simple fact that they were Muslim, at over a dozen colleges, including Yale University and the University of Pennsylvania. See "Bloomberg Stands By Spying on Muslims," *RT,* February 22, 2012, http://rt.com/usa/.

## THE MUSLIM MENACE

1. "Mineta Quits with Parting Shot 20-Year Reign: Key Democrat Leaves Congress, Calls GOP Agenda 'Mean,'" *San Jose Mercury News,* October 8, 1995.

2. Pamela Geller, "Pamela Geller: In Her Own Words," interview, *New York Times,* October 8, 2010, http://www.nytimes.com.

3. Laurie Goodstein, "Drawing U.S. Crowds with Anti-Muslim Message," *New York Times,* March 7, 2011, http://www.nytimes.com.

4. Evan McMorris Santoro, "Gingrich Calls for Federal Ban on Shariah Law in US," *Talking Points Memo,* September 18, 2010, http://tpmdc.talkingpointsmemo.com.

5. Many observant Muslims, similar to Christians in previous centuries, eschew involvement with interest, essentially requiring them to use different banking and financial tools than everyone else. With a billion and a half Muslims in the world, this is clearly an opportunity to

create and sell a whole range of banking products, from checking accounts to mortgage loans, that are "sharia-compliant." Several million Muslims live here in America, many looking for American financial institutions that they can do business with in a way that is consistent with their religious values, a sure-fire market opportunity.

6. Newt and Callista Gingrich, "America at Risk: The War With No Name," *Human Events: Powerful Conservative Voices,* September 8, 2010, http://www.humanevents.com.

7. Reinhold Niebuhr, *The Irony of American History* (Chicago: University of Chicago Press, 1952), xxiv.

8. Lorraine Woellert, "Gingrich Said Freddie Mac Could Be Good Model for Mars Travel," *Bloomberg News,* December 1, 2011, http://www.bloomberg.com.

9. Justin Elliott, "Newt: For Shariah Law Before He Was Against It," *Salon,* June 8, 2011, http://www.salon.com.

10. Newt Gingrich, *Rediscovering God in America: Reflections on the Role of Faith in Our Nation's History and Future* (Ontario: Integrity House, 2006), xiii.

11. Newt Gingrich, "Why I Became a Catholic," *National Catholic Register,* April 26, 2011, www.nationalcatholicregister.com.

12. Newt and Callista Gingrich, "An Inspiring Story of Freedom Through Faith," *Human Events: Powerful Conservative Voices,* April 7, 2010, http://www.humanevents.com.

13. Jerry Filteau, "Pope Made Important Overtures to Non-Christian Religions," *Catholic News Service,* 2005, http://www.catholicnews.com.

14. Maria Monk, *The Awful Disclosures of the Hotel Dieu Monastery in Montreal* (New York, c. 1850), 49.

15. Arthur Schlesinger Jr., *The Disuniting of America: Reflections on a Multicultural Society* (New York: W. W. Norton, 1998), 36.

16. Shaun Casey, *The Making of a Catholic President: Kennedy vs. Nixon 1960* (New York: Oxford University Press, 2009).

## THE EVANGELICAL SHIFT

1. Lydia Saad, "Anti-Muslim Sentiments Fairly Commonplace," Gallup Poll News Service, August 10, 2006, http://media.gallup.com/.

2. Shaun Casey, *The Making of a Catholic President: Kennedy vs. Nixon 1960* (New York: Oxford University Press, 2009).

3. Ibid., 22.

4. Ibid., 168.

5. Mark S. Massa, *Catholics and American Culture: Fulton Sheen, Dorothy Day, and the Notre Dame Football Team* (New York: Crossroad Publishing, 2011), 78.

6. Casey, *The Making of a Catholic President,* 133–34.

7. Ibid., 133.

8. Ibid., 138.

9. Ibid.,125.

10. Massa, *Catholics and American Culture.*

11. Casey, *The Making of a Catholic President,* 141.

12. Ibid.

13. Ibid.

14. Massa, *Catholics and American Culture,* 78.

15. Newt Gingrich, "America at Risk: Camus, National Security and Afghanistan," address, American Enterprise Institute, July 29, 2011, http://www.gingrichproductions.com/.

16. Human Khan and Amy Bingham, "GOP Debate: Newt Gingrich's Comparison of Muslims and Nazi's Sparks Outrage," ABC News, June 13, 2011, http://abcnews.go.com.

17. Tom Hamburger and Matea Gold, "Gingrich Woos Evangelicals as He Eyes Presidential Bid," *Los Angeles Times,* March 3, 2011.

18. Erik Eckholm, "Using History to Mold Ideas on the Right," *New York Times,* May 4, 2011.

19. Jeff Zeleny, "On the Stump, Gingrich Puts Focus on Faith," *New York Times,* February 26, 2011, http://www.nytimes.com.

20. Hamburger and Gold, "Gingrich Woos Evangelicals."

21. Asifa Quaraishi, "Who Says *Shari'a* Demands the Stoning of Women? A Description of Islamic Law and Constitutionalism," *Berkeley Journal of Middle Eastern and Islamic Law* 1 (2008): 163–77, http://www.law.berkeley.edu.

22. Ron Kampeas, "Anti-Sharia Laws Stir Concerns That Halachah Could Be Next," JTA: Global News Service of the Jewish People, April 28, 2011, http://www.jta.org.

23. Justin Elliott, "What Sharia Law Actually Means," *Salon,* February 26, 2011, http://www.salon.com.

24. Investigative Staff of the *Boston Globe, Betrayal: The Crisis in the Catholic Church* (Boston: Little, Brown, 2002).

25. Ibid.

26. Anna Quindlen, *Loud and Clear* (New York: Random House, 2005), 113.

27. *Boston Globe, Betrayal.*

28. Erick Eckholm and Jeff Zeleny, "Evangelicals, Seeking Unity, Back Santorum for Nomination," *New York Times,* January 14, 2012.

29. Drew Katchen, "Graham: Santorum, Gingrich Christians; You Have to Ask Obama If He Is," *Morning Joe,* MSNBC, February 21, 2012, http://mojoe.msnbc.msn.com/.

30. Jonathan Capehart, "Angry Rick Santorum 'Throws Up on JFK,'" *Washington Post,* February 27, 2012.

## THE SCIENCE OF INTERFAITH COOPERATION

1. *This Week with Christiane Amanpour,* ABC-TV, September 28, 2010.

2. Laurie Goodstein, "American Muslims Ask, Will We Ever Belong?" *New York Times,* September 10, 2010, http://www.nytimes.com.

3. Institute for Islamic Thought, "A Common Word Between Us and You," *A Common Word: Official Website,* 2009, http://acommonword.com.

4. Jonathan Sacks, *The Dignity of Difference: How to Avoid the Clash of Civilizations* (New York: Continuum, 2003).

5. Diana Eck, *A New Religious America: How a "Christian Country" Has Become the World's Most Religiously Diverse Nation* (San Francisco: Harper, 2002).

6. Donald G. McNeil, "A $10 Mosquito Net Is Making Charity Cool," *New York Times,* June 2, 2008, http://www.nytimes.com.

7. Robert Putnam, *Bowling Alone: The Collapse and Revival of American Community* (New York: Simon & Schuster, 2000).

8. Robert Putnam, *"E Pluribus Unum:* Diversity and Community in the Twenty-first Century—The 2006 Johan Skytte Prize," *Scandinavian Political Studies* 30, no. 2 (June 2007).

9. Putnam, *Bowling Alone,* 66.

10. Putnam, *"E Pluribus Unum,"* 148–49.

11. Robert Putnam, *Better Together: Restoring the American Community* (New York: Simon & Schuster, 2003).

12. Ashutosh Varshney, *Ethnic Conflict and Civic Life: Hindus and Muslims in India* (New Haven, CT: Yale University Press, 2003).

13. Scott Keeter and Gregory Smith, "Public Opinion about Mormons," Pew Forum on Religion and Public Life, 2007, http://pewresearch.org/.

14. Robert Putnam and David Campbell, *American Grace: How Religion Divides and Unites Us* (New York: Simon & Schuster, 2010).

15. "Views of Religious Similarities and Differences: Muslims Widely Seen as Facing Discrimination," Pew Forum on Religious and Public Life, 2009 Annual Religion and Public Life Survey, http://pewforum.org/.

16. Lydia Saad, "Anti-Muslim Sentiments Fairly Commonplace," Gallup Poll News Service, August 10, 2006, http://media.gallup.com/.

17. Gallup Center for Muslim Studies, "In U.S., Religious Prejudice Stronger Against Muslims," Gallup.com, January 21, 2010, http://www.gallup.com/.

18. Michael Shapiro, *Who Will Teach for America?* (Washington, DC: Farragut, 1993).

19. Wendy Kopp, *One Day, All Children . . . : The Unlikely Triumph of Teach for America and What I Learned Along the Way* (New York: Public Affairs, 2003).

## THE ART OF INTERFAITH LEADERSHIP

1. Chip Heath and Dan Heath, *Switch: How to Change Things When Change Is Hard* (New York: Crown Business Publishing, 2010), 27–32.

2. Ranya Idliby, Suzanne Oliver, and Priscilla Warner, *The Faith Club: A Muslim, a Christian, a Jew—Three Women Search for Understanding* (New York: Free Press, 2006).

3. Eboo Patel, *Acts of Faith: The Story of an American Muslim, the Struggle for the Soul of Generation* (Boston: Beacon, 2007).

4. His Holiness The Dalai Lama, *Toward a True Kinship of Faiths: How the World's Religions Can Come Together* (New York: Doubleday, 2010).

5. Ibid., 79.

6. Chris Stedman, *Faitheist: How an Atheist Found Common Ground with the Religious* (Boston: Beacon, forthcoming).

7. Chris Stedman, "Why This 'Mosque' Matters to Atheists," *Non-Prophet Status,* July 28, 2010, http://nonprophetstatus.wordpress.com/.

8. Tironi quote from National Task Force on Civic Learning and Democratic Engagement, *A Crucible Moment: College Learning and Democracy's Future* (Washington, DC: Association of American Colleges and Universities, 2010), 25.

## COLLEGES

1. "Rabin's Alleged Killer Appears in Court," CNN.com, November 7, 1995.

2. Savva Amusin et al., "Bringing Interfaith to the University of Illinois," *Building the Interfaith Youth Movement: Beyond Dialogue to Action,* Eboo Patel and Patrice Brodeur, eds. (Lanham, MD: Rowman & Littlefield, 2006).

3. Diana Eck, *Encountering God: A Spiritual Journey from Bozeman to Banaras* (Boston: Beacon, 1993).

4. Alexander and Helen Astin's official website, *Spirituality in Higher Education,* may be found at http://spirituality.ucla.edu/.

5. National Task Force on Civic Learning and Democratic Engagement, *A Crucible Moment: College Learning and Democracy's Future,* (Washington, DC: Association for American Colleges and Universities, 2011), 18.

6. Acts 17:26.

7. John G. Fee, *Autobiography of John G. Fee* (Berea, KY: National Christian Association, 1981).

## SEMINARIES

1. Andrea Elliott, "A Bloody Crime in New Jersey Divides Egyptians," *New York Times,* January 21, 2005, http://www.nytimes.com.

2. Wilfred Cantwell Smith, *The Faith of Other Men* (New York: Harper Torchbooks, 1962), 94–96.

3. Christian Smith, *Soul Searching: The Religious and Spiritual Lives of American Teenagers* (New York: Oxford University Press, 2005).

4. Kenda Creasy Dean, *Almost Christian: What the Faith of Our Teenagers Is Telling the American Church* (New York: Oxford University Press, 2010).

5. Diana Eck, "Preface," in *Encountering God: A Spiritual Journey from Bozeman to Banaras* (Boston: Beacon, 1993).

6. Luke 10:25.

7. John 4:1–27.

8. Sura 96:1.

9. Montgomery Watt, *Muhammad: Prophet and Statesman* (New York: Oxford University Press, 1974).

10. Martin Luther King Jr. and Clayborne Carson, *The Autobiography of Martin Luther King, Jr.* (New York: Warner Books, 1998).

11. Clayborne Carson, ed., *The Papers of Martin Luther King, Jr.: Volume V: The Threshold of a New Decade* (Berkeley: University of California Press, 2005).

12. Susannah Heschel, "Following in My Father's Footsteps: Selma 40 Years Later," *VOX on Dartmouth: The Newspaper for Dartmouth Faculty and Staff,* April 4, 2005, http://www.dartmouth.edu.

13. Ibid.

14. King, *The Autobiography of Martin Luther King, Jr.,* 23.

## AMERICAN MUSLIM CHILD

1. David Foster Wallace, *This Is Water: Some Thoughts, Delivered on a Significant Occasion, about Living a Compassionate Life* (New York: Little, Brown, 2009).

2. James Baldwin, *Notes of a Native Son* (Boston: Beacon, 1955).

3. Chaim Potok, *The Book of Lights* (Robinsdale, MN: Fawcett, 1982).

4. Demi, *Muhammad* (New York: Margaret K. McElderry, 2003).

## CONCLUSION

1. William Saletan, "Christian Terrorism," *Slate,* July 25, 2011, http://www.slate.com.

2. Wajahat Ali et al., *Fear, Inc.: The Roots of the Islamophobia Network in America,* Center for American Progress, August 2011, http://www.americanprogress.org/.

3. Taylor Branch, *Pillar of Fire: America in the King Years, 1963–65* (New York: Simon & Schuster, 1999).

4. Scott Shane, "Killings in Norway Spotlight Anti-Muslim Thought in U.S." *New York Times,* July 24, 2011.

5. Mark Jurgensmeyer, "Why Breivik Was a Christian Terrorist," *Huffington Post,* July 7, 2011, http://www.huffingtonpost.com.

6. Psalms 137:8–9.

7. William Blake, "The Little Black Boy," stanza 4, in *Songs of Innocence,* 1789–1790.

8. Clayborne Carson, ed., *The Papers of Martin Luther King, Jr.: Volume V: The Threshold of a New Decade* (Berkeley: University of California Press, 2005).

# INDEX

Ground Zero mosque. *See* Cordoba House

Hamdani, Mohammad Salman, 11–12
Hamza Yusuf, Shaykh, xxiii–xxv
Hannity, Sean, 31
Hanson, Mark. *See* Hamza Yusuf, Shaykh
Hart, Edward, 13, 14
Heath, Chip and Dan, 89
Heschel, Abraham Joshua, 151, 164
Hitchens, Christopher, xi
Hodgson, Roger, 13
Hornady, Margaret, 129
Hughes, Langston, 17
Hutaree, 164

IFYC. *See* Interfaith Youth Core (IFYC)
Immigration Act of 1965, 17, 137
Ingraham, Laura, xviii
interfaith cooperation. *See* interfaith work
Interfaith in Action, 122–23
interfaith literacy, 86, 93, 95–97, 120, 166
interfaith triangle, 86, 92–94, 101, 124
interfaith work: art of interfaith cooperation, 101–2; college campuses' role in, 102–3; consideration of the effectiveness of, xxvi–xxvii; example of an Evangelical's support of Muslims (*see* Roberts, Bob); examples of interfaith leadership, 165–69; growth in, worldwide, 68–71; IFYC and (*see* Interfaith Youth Core); interfaith cooperation and Cordoba House, 91; involving young people in,

70–71; meaning of interfaith, 138; mistake of presenting as science, 86–87; motivations for getting involved in, 91–92; and need for focus on building relationships and knowledge, 80; one person's path to interfaith leadership, 98–101; percentage of Americans who view Islam as different from their religion, xi; "preaching to the choir" as strategy for effectiveness in, 88–90, 93–94, 97; and reciprocity regarding how peoples' rights are respected, 17–19, 22; and view that religious prejudice is un-American, 68
Interfaith Youth Core (IFYC): approach to fund-raising, 71–72; critique of program's effectiveness, 81–83; focus of, xi–xii, 84–85, 124; framework for pluralism, 71; inspiration of Cordoba, xiii; questions about effectiveness, 66–67, 73–74; success in involving young people, 69–71; view that young people are committed to being bridge builders, 121
Iowa Republican caucus, 48–49
Islam. *See* Muslims in America
Islamic Free Market Institute, 34
Islamophobia, 19, 22, 30–32, 46, 55, 163, 165

Jackson, Jesse, 15–16, 17
Japanese American Citizens League, 18
Jersey City, New Jersey, 132
Jewish Telegraphic Agency, 50
Jews, 14, 50